1525.

PLANTS OF THE BALEARIC ISLANDS

ANTHONY BONNER

PLANTS OF THE BALEARIC ISLANDS

Illustrations by HANNAH BONNER

Translated from the Catalan
by Patricia Mathews

EDITORIAL MOLL
MALLORCA
1992

EDITORIAL MOLL
Torre de l'Amor, 4
07001 Palma de Mallorca

The author wishes to express his thanks to Jesús R. Jurado for permission to use photographs number 1, 2, 3, 4, 5, 8, 9, 11, 12, 13, 14, 17, 19 and 20, to Francesc Moll Marquès for number 6, 7, 10, 15 and 16, and to Lleonard Llorens for number 18.

Depòsit Legal: B. 317-1992
I.S.B.N. 84-273-0423-4

Imprès a Sirven Gràfic
Santander, 60-62
08020 Barcelona

PROLOGUE TO THE ENGLISH EDITION

Dreams never come true the way the dreamer would have liked them to. The original Catalan edition of this book began as a single chapter of a more ambitious book on all of Balearic natural history, a book which was to be written jointly by members of the Grup Balear d'Ornitologia i de Defensa de la Naturalesa and the local Natural History Society. But we ran up against the bugbear of all joint efforts: some collaborators with less enthusiasm than others, or with less time. It was going to be a long drawn-out process, and faced with the alternative of publishing an incomplete manuscript or waiting several years for all the chapters to be completed, we hit upon a third possibility: publishing the original book as a series of shorter, self-contained volumes, of which this was merely the first to appear. Since then it has been joined by two excellent companion volumes, that by Joan Mayol Serra on the birds, and that by Josep Antoni Alcover on the mammals of the Balearics. We hope soon to be able to add one on reptiles and amphibians, another on geology, another... But it's best not to make too many promises. It all depends on whether our collaborators can find the necessary time.

This book — like others in the series — is intended for the general public. Its purpose is to help the beginner find his way. It is for the hiker, the amateur botanist, the nature-lover, or the ordinary person who wants to know what he's seeing when he strolls through the woods. It's a book to take with you into the country rather than to place on the bookshelf. That's why we've included numerous illustrations and photographs.

A second purpose in writing this book — one both more personal and, at the time of writing, less conscious — was to explain to myself the singular and yet varied beauty of the Balearic landscape. What is it that gives a particular piece of mountain scree, oak forest or rocky coast its special character? What is it that makes it so different from equivalent bits of scenery in northern Europe or North America, or even elsewhere in the Mediterranean? This is why I have gone a bit into plant communities, since in many ways they hold the key to such visual and aesthetic differences. And if I can help explain these beauties to the traveller in these islands, and persuade him of how much more there is here than the cement blocks of hotels, apartment houses, shops and discothèques which disfigure some parts of the coast, I will be more than satisfied.

Now in a book of this sort, I naturally have had to limit myself to the most common, characteristic or interesting plants, and this has obliged me to make a fairly subjective choice from among the 1,500 (approximately) species which are to be found in the Balearics. I have included no cultivated plants, nor any plants which were introduced by man — with the exception of a few which have adapted so thoroughly to the local environment that they could well be considered indigenous (olive, sorrel, etc.).

One last word — or rather a plea. Everything on the Balearic Islands is on a smaller scale than elsewhere, and this applies to the number of specimens of rarer flowers. There are some species that grow only in an area that measures 30 x 30 yards, and when I say "only", I mean in the entire world. Don't assume that if you see only two or three specimens of a particular plant in one spot, that there will be many others elsewhere. All too often on these islands there is no elsewhere. In the mistaken assumption that nature was endlessly self-replenishing, botanists caused the Silene hifacense to disappear from the coasts of Valencia (see p. 103), nature lovers have almost eradicated the lady's slipper, Europe's most beautiful orchid, from its Continental and British habitats, and it may well be that the near-disappearance of Minorca's Vicia bifoliolata (see p. 103) can be blamed on collectors of rare plants. Thank goodness, as Polunin says, for the modern single-lens reflex camera and for color-slides, which permit plants to be "collected" without being killed. And what better light than that of the Mediterranean for carrying out this kind of "collecting"?

There only remains the pleasant job of thanking the friends who have helped me with this book. First among them is Father Francesc Bonafè, who guided me and answered so many of my questions as I became increasingly interested in the botany of the Balearic Islands. He let me consult his splendid Flora de Mallorca (see no. 13 in the Bibliography at the end of this book) while it was still in typescript, and he kindly read the manuscript of this book, saving me from a number of botanical errors. Antoni and Lleonard Llorens did likewise, and, in addition, gave me permission to use some of their color photographs, as did Jesús R. Jurado. The delicate job of editing the original Catalan text (and correcting my many errors) was patiently done by Francesc Moll Marquès and his sister, Catalina. And if I have been able to delineate the plant communities of these islands with such assurance, it is because I have been able to follow the fundamental geobotanical studies of Oriol de Bolòs (see no. 19 in the Bibliography).

For this English edition, in addition to being able to make use of Vols. 4-5 of the Flora Europaea to bring my botanical nomenclature up to date, I have the added pleasant task of thanking the friends who helped me bring other information up to date. First of all there is Guillem Alomar, who provided me with two long lists of new citations and localities; then there is Guillem Orfila Pons, who provided a wealth of new information concerning Minorca, some based on his own discoveries, and some based on those of his friends Andreu Bermejo and Antoni Gómez; then Cristòfol Guerau d'Arellano and Nestor Torres corrected many details and brought me up to date on the flowers of Ibiza. Lleonard Llorens, now head of the Botany Department of the islands' new university, once again did me the favor of reading through the entire book and making countless invaluable suggestions and corrections. Lastly, Franklyn H. Perring, one of the contributors to Flora Europaea, very kindly read through the entire English translation and caught hundreds of oversights, inacccuracies and unidiomatic turns of phrase which had slipped through the hands of an author who had learned what little botany he knew in a language other than English. To all my sincerest thanks. Without undue modesty, I can say that whatever degree of reliability this book may have is very largely due to them.

WOODS AND SCRUB

Introduction

When we go out into the Majorcan countryside we are all aware of the differences in the landscape: the green of cultivated fields, the shade of the oak forest, the brilliant light of seaside dunes, the poor, stone-covered mountain lands, the cliffs surprisingly spotted with vegetation, the rocky coasts which endure suffocating heat in the summer and the battering of the sea in winter, or the eternally damp marshlands. All these landscapes differ visually and aesthetically from one another because differences in the amount of sun, in their location, in their history, or in their microclimate have given birth to different communities of plants. Or, to put it another way, the vegetation always has to overcome some disadvantage or problem, some excess or shortage (of sun, heat, water, wind, salt, drainage, etc.). This has given rise to myriad adaptations, to plants that have managed to circumvent a handicap or turn it to profit, sometimes to such an extent that the plant has become dominant in a specific habitat or unable to live in any other. These problems of excess or shortage may provide us a key to understanding the vegetation around us, to identifying the plant communities of the Balearic Islands.

For this reason we must begin with the basic fact that the Balearic Islands are part of the Mediterranean, and not just the Mediterranean in its strictly geographic sense, but also including the entire surrounding area which has similarities of climate and vegetation. As we can see from Map 1, this includes very little of Atlantic and central Europe and only that part of North Africa which is not the Sahara; on the other hand, it includes a considerable part of the Black Sea coast.

Within this area the vegetation must confront a basic problem: the almost constant heat and dryness of the three summer months of June, July and August. The biological effect of this period is comparable to that of the Northern winter. In both cases plants must devise innumerable ways to survive. The simplest, but most violent solution, is to die in the difficult season. In the case of annuals the entire plant disappears, leaving only the seed with its minimum requirements as to temperature and moisture. In the case of perennials, the entire visible part of the plant may die while the underground part survives, often in the form of a bulb or corm, protected by a layer of soil (asphodel, arum, etc.) or only the leaves may die (thorny broom, *Anthyllis cytisoides*). So here, as in the north, in the hard season we have the sight of desolate lands which look half-burned, with that *café-au-lait* color of wilted vegetation and barren soil. And then, just as in the north, where all it takes is a little bit of warmth as the days grow longer for the greenery to burst forth, so here, all it takes is a bit of water as days begin to shorten. The Majorcans are so aware of this similarity that the word "autumn" does not exist in their language. Instead, they speak of two springs: a "summer" one and a "winter" one.

The almost complete lack of deciduous trees in the Mediterranean region also plays a part here. In the North, all the trees (except conifers and a few evergreens) lose their leaves when faced with winter's threat of freezing their tender tissues. Here, by contrast, the trees must profit from the rainy season, keeping their leaves in order to do their job of photosynthesizing those substances (particularly water itself) which can be drawn from the soil only during this time of year. Thus, while the northern forest is at the height of its greenness in summer, here it is at its peak in mid-winter when the rains have washed it clean of summer's dust.

On the other hand, Mediterranean vegetation has made a series of adaptations to the heat and dryness which are without parallel in the North. There exist some mechanisms, such as enormously long roots, for extracting water from deeper in the soil (every Majorcan knows how the roots of fig trees can spread to crack wells a considerable distance away) and others, such as succulence, for storing water (stone crop and prickly pear).

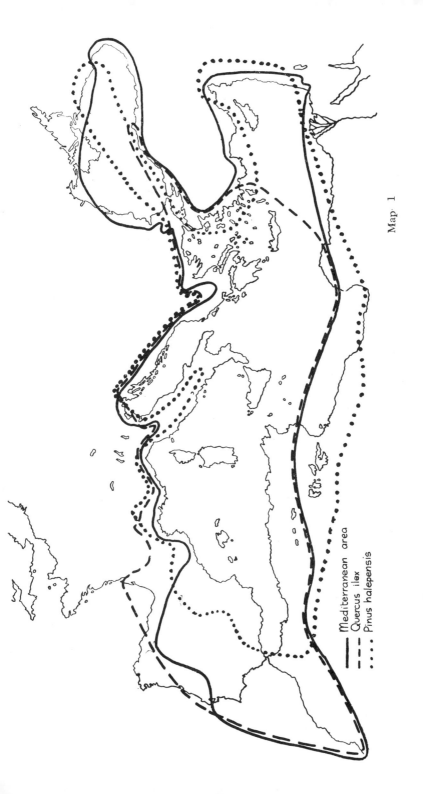

Map 1

——— Mediterranean area
– – – Quercus ilex
· · · · Pinus halepensis

But the most important are a series of adaptations which reduce the leaves' transpiration rate and keep water loss to a
minimum. One way to achieve this is by reducing the size of
the leaf (as in the case of the olive tree). In some cases (the
asparagus), the leaf disappears altogether; in others (rosemary,
everlasting, heather), the edges curl up, reducing the leaf's
surface. Some leaves keep transpiration down with a harder, more
impermeable outer layer —botanists call these "coriaceous" leaves
(the olive, the holm oak, the carob)— others with a waxy or resinous covering (aromatic inula, narrow-leaved cistus). There are
also plants with a covering of fine hairs (grey-leaved cistus, kidney-
vetch) which helps preserve spaces of still air, thus slowing down
the interchange of vapor with the atmosphere.

There are plants which have vertical, rather than horizontal,
leaf blades in orden to keep the sun from hitting them straight
on. The best known of these plants is the eucalyptus which forms
the famous "forests without shade" of its native Australia by
twisting the leaf-stem. Butcher's broom does likewise (although,
as you will see from p. 41, in this case they are not strictly leaves
as such) as, to a certain extent do species of daphne. *Cneorum
tricoccon* turns its petiole upward, maintaining the entire leaf in
a vertical position.

Trees

The simplest and most logical way of avoiding transpiration
is by making shade, and the most important and typical plant
community of our part of the Mediterranean, the oak forest or
Quercion ilicis, as it is called by scientists (see p. 60) manages
to do that extremely well. So let us look at its main plants, beginning, naturally enough, with the plant which gives the community
its name, the holm oak (*Quercus ilex*). This tree seldom reaches a
height of more than 15 metres, but in exceptional cases has been
known to grow to heights of 20-25 metres (see p. 17 for one
located close to Palma). As we mentioned earlier, the leaves are
quite coriaceous and have a multitude of shapes: sometimes on a

single tree one can find leaves that are spiny or entire, large or small, round or narrow. They also vary in colour, but not so much so: normally (but see the next page) the top part of the leaf is green and the underside a greyish colour.

From time immemorial the holm oak has had three commercial uses: the acorns for pigs, the wood for making charcoal, and the bark for its high tannin content, used in tanning hides and in setting dyes. The presence of tannin has also made for dozens of medicinal uses (which the reader will find described in Palau i Ferrer's excellent publication: see Bibliography).

As will be seen in Map 1, the holm oak is largely to be found in the Mediterranean area: the only exceptions are its absence from the Near East and its occurrence in the areas bordering the Bay of Biscay.

A very close relation —so close, in fact, that many botanists consider it a sub-species or variety [1]— is the *Quercus rotundifolia* which differs principally in the sweet taste of the acorn (the acorn of the holm oak is bitter). This tree does not appear to be indigenous to the Balearic Islands (except possibly Ibiza). Usually only isolated examples are to be found and they are almost certainly the result of grafts.

Another close relation is the kermes oak (*Quercus coccifera*), easily confused with the young holm oak. It's the runt of the family, usually taking the form of a bush one or two metres tall. It is distinguished from the holm oak by the cup of its acorn which has pricklier scales, and particularly by the leaves which

---

[1] The reader might be helped here by a few words of explanation about the classification system used by biologists. The basic category is the *species* which can be defined —simplifying considerably— as a group of individuals which share and reproduce the same characteristics and do not usually mix with individuals of other groups. Species which have a series of common characteristics make up a *genus,* the genera make up *families* and so on through *orders, classes,* etc. The species itself may be divided into varieties and still further into forms. Thus, the biological categories are as follows (ranging from the most general to the most specific): kingdom, division, class, order, family, genus, species, variety, form. Furthermore, each of these categories can be divided into sub-kingdoms, sub-divisions, etc. However, in this book we generally use only a few of this deluge of names: family, genus, species, sub-species (abbreviated as ssp.) and variety (var. or v.).

are spinier, and green on the underside rather than greyish like those of the holm oak. But be careful to study mature leaves because sometimes the young leaves of the holm oak have not yet developed that microscopic fuzziness which gives them their greyish hue.

In olden times the bush was of great economic importance as it was the host of the scale insect *Coccus ilicis*, the female of which was collected when immobilized on the branches in the form of a gall, dried and used as the base for a scarlet dye. The word "kermes" comes from the Arab as does the word for the dye: "carmine".

The area in which the kermes oak grows coincides even more closely with the Mediterranean area than does the holm oak. A surprising exception is most of Italy where it is found only on "the heel of the boot" and the southern part of Sicily. Its distribution in the Balearic Islands is also odd. It abounds only on Ibiza. It doesn't exist at all in Minorca, and on Majorca it is limited to isolated spots located within a triangle formed by Palma-Esporles-Andratx, a couple of places between Lluc-major and Felanitx, and a few examples around Artà and Santa Maria. The reader who wants to see it in the city of Palma will find it growing in abundance in the hills behind the hotel Son Vida.

All the foregoing species of oak are evergreen, with leaves that last two or three years. The same holds true of the cork oak (*Quercus suber*), of which only isolated examples, introduced by man, are to be found in the Balearic Islands.[2] The only deciduous tree of this genus to be found in these islands is the Lusitanian oak, *Quercus faginea* (= *Q. lusitanica* ssp. *valentina*) (**111**) of Ibero-Mauritanian distribution. Examples may be seen in Puigpunyent on the hill known as Puig des Reures beside the stream near the entrance to the village or in the gardens at Es Salt at the opposite end of the town. There is some disagreement about whether its

---

[2] With the possible exception of Minorca, where specimens (including young vigorous ones) have been found growing within holm oak forests in some half a dozen places.

presence is "a relic of the Ice Age in the islands" as Colom says, or if it was introduced by man. The only certain fact is that it was first mentioned by A. Furió in his book, *Panorama óptico-histórico-artístico de las Islas Baleares,* 1840 (or 1844).

The reader interested in seeing these five species of *Quercus* will find them all on the Palma-Puigpunyent road. Holm oaks are everywhere. Kermes oaks are to be found at kilometre 10, at the top of the rise in the road after the Son Marill Bridge. There are two cork oaks at K. 13 next to the houses of Son Puig, and just before entering the village, next to a little bridge over the stream, there are two magnificent *Quercus faginea.* The best place to see a *Quercus rotundifolia* is behind the houses of Son Net, below the Molí Nou. There you will find what I believe to be the most majestic holm oak in all Majorca: it is so well known that you have only to ask any villager for "s'alzina grossa" (the big oak).

Certainly the most abundant tree in the Balearic Islands is the Aleppo pine (*Pinus halepensis*). It grows anywhere from beside the sea to an altitude of about a thousand metres in the mountains. When blessed with a good location it is capable of growing into a tree with a straight trunk some twenty metres tall. On the other hand, in windy coastal or mountain areas it may take on twisted shapes, sometimes with the trunk growing completely parallel to the ground. The most curious deformation is known locally as "witch's graft", produced by a parasitic fungus, which causes a portion of the tree to grow into a spherical shape, much denser and thicker than the rest of the tree.

From time immemorial good use has been made of the pine: the wood in shipbuilding, the branches for burning in ovens and the resin for making pitch. It is worth noting that the shape of the tree we are accustomed to seeing (with a slim, entirely bare trunk) is due to the lower branches being cut for use in bread-ovens; normally the pine is sturdier and rounder. Now that ships are built of steel and fibre glass, and ovens are run by gas or electricity, we will begin to see denser, possibly more beautiful forests, but they will certainly be more prone to forest fires as well.

Because of its sensitivity to cold the pine is to be found almost strictly in the Mediterranean (see Map 1). Its other great enemy is the caterpillar of a kind of gypsy moth, *Thaumetopoea pityocampa,* which has done considerable damage in some parts of the Islands.

There are two other pines in the Balearic Islands. The first is the stone pine or umbrella pine *(Pinus pinea)* which is rare and was probably introduced by man. It is less rare in Ibiza and is said to have been abundant there long ago. It is a very decorative tree with its straight naked trunk topped by umbrella-shaped branches. It also yields the pine nuts which are widely used in cooking.

The other pine was recently discovered near the coast of Llucmajor by Antoni and Lleonard Llorens, who christened it *Pinus halepensis,* v. *ceciliae.* It is immediately distinguishable from the common pine by its branches, which grow much more vertically upward, giving the tree a cypress-like appearance. Since its first discovery, other specimens have been found near Artà, on Minorca (principally near the south coast) and on Ibiza. At present studies are under way to establish the status of this interesting new variety.

Two of the most important trees in the Balearic Islands are species which have been domesticated by man: the olive *(Olea europea)* and the carob *(Ceratonia siliqua).* We know that the olive was first cultivated in the Middle East, spread as far as Greece in pre-Homeric times, was introduced into Italy by Greek colonists and from there spread to Gaul and the north of Spain. Further south, it was almost certainly the Phoenicians who introduced it into North Africa, southern Hispania and the Balearic Islands (see Map 2). But, remember, we're talking about the *cultivated* olive tree. What we don't know is whether the tree previously existed in a wild state throughout the Mediterranean area. Many botanists believe it did, and that would explain the existence of what appear to be three varieties of olive tree: the cultivated tree (var. *europea* or *sativa*), the "wild" olive (var. *silvestris*) and, lastly, the thorny little var. *oleaster,* a bush with square branches and tiny leaves which could be the true vestige of the origi-

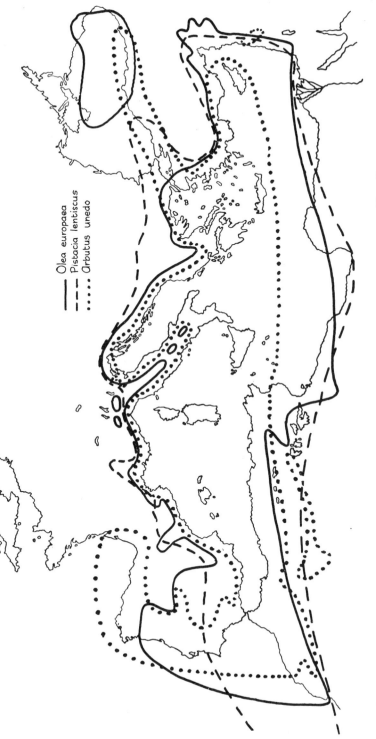

Olea europaea
Pistacia lentiscus
Arbutus unedo

Map 2

nal plant. However, this is no more than a hypothesis (there is not always such a clear distinction between var. *silvestris* and var. *oleaster*). These wild varieties are found in places which could not possibly be remains of plantations. Still, the trees might conceivably be fugitives from cultivation which have become naturalized. They are almost always found in habitats which are characterized by aridity and strong sun, and associated with the carob described below and with other species to form the plant community known as *Oleo-Ceratonion* which we will describe later on.

Many have sung of the olive's beauty, but few have taken time to rhapsodize over its companion, the carob (*Ceratonia siliqua*). Looked at objectively, however, it is a very beautiful tree, with thick, shiny foliage which is frequently two-toned (because the young leaves are a lighter green) and with a trunk which is often as fantastically gnarled as that of an olive. It is also an unusual tree in many ways. It is the only species of its genus in the entire world, which indicates that the species is a relic of a far distant past. The tiny petal-less blossoms may be male (with nothing but the five stamens), female (with only the pistil which looks like an embryo carob) and, more rarely, hermaphrodite. A tree is usually entirely masculine or entirely feminine, but mixtures do exist. The flowers and, consequently, the fruit sprout from the midst of the branch, often in old, very woody, parts, and sometimes even from the trunk itself. But no matter how black and hard these carobs may be, they contain surprisingly over 50% sugar. The tree is capable of growing in conditions of unbelievable aridity and heat. I've read of large specimens in Sicily which grow in almost solid rock, rock which is made so hot by the sun that a person could not touch it.

As a final, curious detail, it is said that the seed gave jewelers their unit of weight: the carat. This is not completely certain, but it is true that the Catalan word *quirat*, the Spanish *quilate*, the French and English *carat* and others all come from the Greek *keration*, the name of the carob itself (and origin of the tree's scientific name) and that this Greek word is the diminutive of *keras*, "horn" the name given the fruit because of its long, curved shape. Though this tree was introduced by man, it has become a natural feature of the entire Mediterranean, and grows spontaneously in the hottest, driest parts of our islands.

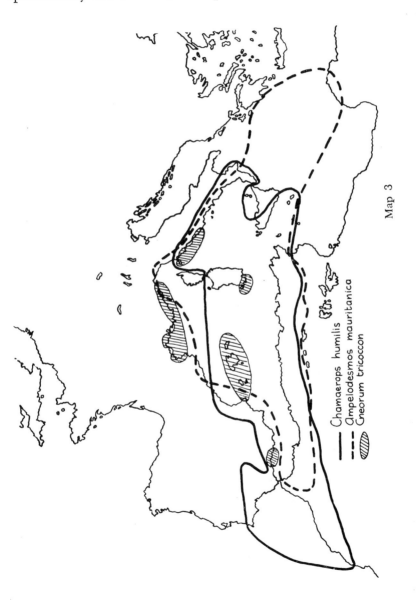

Map 3

Chamaerops humilis
Ampelodesmos mauritanica
Cneorum tricoccon

Within Balearic woodlands we also find a diminutive tree, the dwarf fan palm (*Chamaerops humilis*). This is the only palm tree native to Europe, where it is limited to Spain, Italy and the islands in between (see Map 3). In the Balearic Islands it is oddly distributed: it is found in three separate parts of Majorca with only occasional intervening specimens; in Ibiza and Formentera it grows on the coastal cliffs and in Minorca it grows sparsely on the north coast and in the interior (see Map 4). Its size varies greatly, ranging from small specimens with leaves that seem to emerge straight from the ground to old ones with trunks more than two metres tall (the biggest ones I've seen are in Canyamel and in the woods at Formentor). Long ago the dwarf fan palm was an important feature of Majorcan cottage industry. The leaves were dried in the sun and braided to make cord which was used to weave all sorts of chairs and baskets.[3]

The Commoner Shrubs

Although there are few species of trees (only the five previously mentioned: holm oak, pine, olive, carob and dwarf fan palm) and annuals in Balearic woodlands and scrub, they are very rich in shrubs. First among them is surely the mastic tree or lentisk (*Pistacia lentiscus*) (see Map 2) which is the most common and best known of them all. It is one of the most adaptable plants of the Balearic Islands: we find it at the seaside and high in the mountains, in extremely arid zones and next to rushing streams. According to Barceló y Combis, the peasants of bygone days used to extract an oil from the fruit which they used in lamps as the Arabs do. It is popularly believed that if you keep a sprig of mastic between your lips while you go walking you'll feel refreshed even on the hottest day. This probably stems from the pleasant resinous scent the plant gives off in the summer. In the Greek islands the tree is cultivated for its sap which is extracted through

---

[3] For a good description of this work see the book by the Archduke Luis Salvador, *Costumbres de los Mallorquines*, Vol. II, pages 165-169.

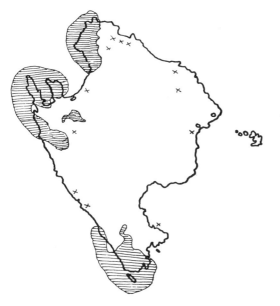

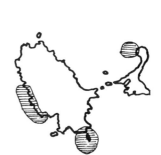

area of distribution

x   isolated specimens

Map 4. Chamaerops humilis

incisions in the trunk and which yields the mastic used in varnish, perfumes, liqueurs and jams. Ever since the remote past the center of production has been, as the medieval Catalan chronicler Muntaner puts it, "the island of Chios, which is a very delightful island and the only place in the world where mastic is produced". The mastic tree comes from a family (the *Anacardiaceae*) rich in exotic resins. It includes the lacquer trees of the Far East (particularly the *Rhus vernicifera*) and the bushes which give the biblical myrrh (*Commiphora abyssinica*) and incense (*Boswelli carteri*). In North America there are two species of *Rhus* (sumac and poison ivy) with resin so poisonous that a mere touch of it on the skin is enough to produce inflammation or intense irritation.

In Majorca the mastic has a related species — the *Pistacia terebinthus* or turpentine tree. Although this plant is not rare elsewhere in the Mediterranean, it exists only as a relic in the Balearic Islands (there are a few examples around Puig de Maçanella and the Gorg Blau). It differs from the mastic in that it is deciduous, has a terminal leaflet (or, as botanists say, its leaf is imparipinnate), and many of its branches end in a group of large horns which look like fruit, but which are actually galls caused by aphids.

The bush which gives the genus its name and produces the fruit used in sweets and ice creams is the pistachio (*Pistacia vera*). It is a native of Asia and cultivated in southern Europe. It used to be cultivated in Minorca and Ibiza, where some specimens are still to be found.

Perhaps the most beautiful shrub of the Balearic forests is the strawberry tree (*Arbutus unedo*) (**1**) with its large shiny leaves, the green of which are in striking contrast to the reddish branches. It is especially lovely in October and November when the clusters of bell-shaped white flowers bloom simultaneously with the ripening of the fruit which is first orange and finally a deep red color. We find them together because, curiously enough, the fruit takes almost exactly a year to ripen, so this year's fruit is the result of last year's flower. The fruit is edible, but doesn't have much flavor. It is said that its Latin name *unedo* meant "eat one", implying that one is quite enough. The plant (see Map 2) has a

Mediterranean distribution which extends along the Atlantic coasts and includes, surprisingly, two areas in Ireland. In the Balearic Islands the plant usually seeks cool spots, frequently growing on the northern slopes of hills.

1. *Arbutus unedo.* Strawberry tree.   2. *Erica multiflora.*

The strawberry tree belongs to the *Ericacae* or heather family, one of the main representatives of which in the Balearics is *Erica multiflora* (2). The family resemblance is evident mostly in the bell shape of the flowers, for the heather's leaf looks more like that of a pine. But here, the needle shape is due to the way the edges of the leaf roll under until they are almost touching (see p. 14). It flowers at the same time as the strawberry tree and, together with the fields of daisies (see p. 57), gives our autumn woods their only note of colour. The plant is used to make light thatching to shade terraces (sheaves are gathered, placed closely together on a support and lashed fast with rope).

A related plant is tree heather (*Erica arborea*). It differs in that it grows considerably taller (two metres is average and it can reach three) blooms in spring (but, beware, the odd *multiflora* sometimes blooms in spring as well) and, when the flowers are open the anthers are almost completely hidden in the corolla (they extend outside the corolla in the *multiflora* and, because they are a blackish purple colour, give a darker tone to that inflorescence). In Catalonia the roots of tree heather are used (or exported to England) to make, the highest quality briar pipes. There is not enough tree heather in the Balearic Islands to support a similar industry: in Majorca and Ibiza the plant is much rarer and more localized than the *Erica multiflora;* in Minorca it abounds in the coastal areas of the north, but is still fairly localized; and it does not exist at all in Cabrera or Formentera.

Green heather (*Erica scoparia*) is found fairly frequently in the humid valleys in the north of Minorca. It differs from tree heather in that the young leaves are smooth (and not velvety), the flower tends to be greenish (rather than pink or white) and has no appendages at the base of the anthers (which, in the case of both plants, are hidden in the corolla). It also tends to bloom somewhat later; tree heather blooms between March and May and green heather between May and July.

A shrub which also grows into a small tree is the Mediterranean buckthorn, *Rhamnus alaternus.* But it is neither very common nor very easy for the beginner to identify. The alternate leaves vary considerably in size, with margins that may be either almost smooth or saw-toothed. But if we look at the leaf against the light, we will see that the margin has a translucent fringe. The flowers, which bloom in February and March, are small, greenish yellow and without petals. The more ill-humored botanical texts state that the wood gives off an unpleasant odour.

Another kind of buckthorn is the *Rhamnus ludovici-salvatoris* (Photo 1), named after a nineteenth-century resident of Majorca who wrote extensively about the islands, the Archduke Luis Salvador of Austria-Hungary. This shrub generally grows to a height of three to five feet, and looks like a dwarf oak with its small serrated, or even spiny, leaves, with their silvery undersides. It is highly decorative, compact and often so symmetrical that it looks as though it had been deliberately trimmed by a gardener. It is of botanical interest principally because it is endemic to, or an endemism of, the Balearic Islands, which means that it exists nowhere else in the world. In this case it is further limited to the northwestern mountain range of Majorca, Cabrera, and, to a more limited extent, Minorca.

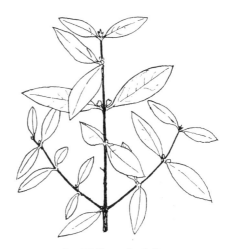

3. *Phillyrea angustifolia.*   4. *Phillyrea latifolia.*

Of the genus *Phillyrea* there are two species in the Balearic Islands: the *Phillyrea angustifolia* (3) with leaves narrower than 10 mm. wide, and the *Phillyrea latifolia* (4) with leaves wider than 15 mm.[4] Both of these shrubs resemble the wild olive (they belong to the same family, the *Oleaceae*), but have longer, more widely spaced leaves. They are fairly common, particularly in the drier, sunnier woods.

Another attractive shrub to be found in Mediterranean woods is myrtle (*Myrtus communis*) (5). This usually grows to a height of one or two metres, although it may reach as many as four or

---

[4] Many authors identify a third —the *P. media*— but the *Flora Europaea* states that this is only a form of the *P. latifolia.*

five metres. The fragrant white blossoms with the multitude of stamens sprout singly from the axil of the leaves and the fruit is blackish (or white, depending upon the variety). But it is the leaves which help most in identifying the myrtle. They are opposite, shiny and of a somewhat oval shape. If we examine them against the light and through a magnifying glass we will see a number of small translucent spots. These are glands of an oily essence which give off a delicious sweet lemony fragrance when the leaf is crushed between the fingers. It is the only member of its family, the *Myrtaceae*, indigenous to Europe. Another member of the family, the eucalyptus, also has oliferous glands in the leaves (which are used for medicinal purposes). The leaves, together with the bark and flowers of the myrtle yield an oil known as "Eau d'Anges" which is used in perfumes. The fruit of certain varieties of myrtle is edible, and formerly the Majorcans used to graft myrtles

5. *Myrtus communis.* Myrtle.
6. *Juniperus oxycedrus.* Prickly juniper, cade.

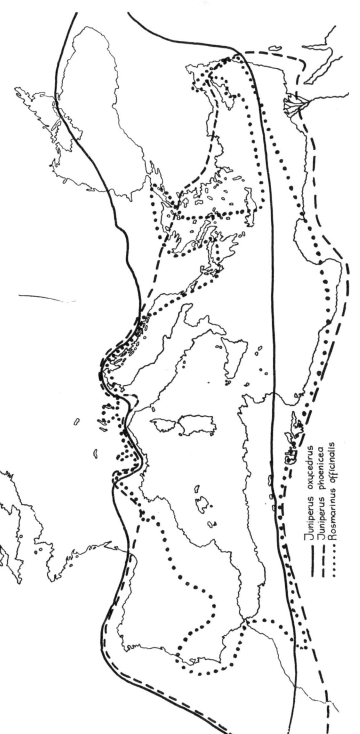

Juniperus oxycedrus
Juniperus phoenicea
Rosmarinus officinalis

Map 5

in order to obtain still sweeter fruit which were a great favorite with children. But this shrub is mostly famous as a symbol of love and peace and as the sacred tree of Venus in classic times. Winners of the Olympic games were crowned with myrtle wreaths as were the poets and playwrites of ancient Rome. We know that it has been cultivated for millenia and thus it is hard to determine its original, natural habitat. But in the Balearic Islands, as in a large part of the Mediterranean, it certainly appears to be indigenous. It is most frequent in Minorca where the climate is rainier. In Majorca it is somewhat more localized in stream beds and in damp shady valleys (although this is not always the case). In Ibiza it is still more rare and localized.

Within the cypress family we have cultivated cypresses and two species of juniper on the seaside dunes (see p. 120); but in the interior of the islands the only wild variety to be found is *Juniperus oxycedrus* (6) (See Map 5). Absolutely no *Juniperus communis* at all is to be found in the Balearic Islands, which, together with Crete and Spitzbergen (other unfortunate islands that are obliged to use substitutes for manufacturing gin), are the only places in Europe where the common juniper is not to be found.

Juniperus oxycedrus, prickly juniper or cade, is easy to identify with its pointed leaves that grow in groups of three, each one with two fine white lines on the upper side. (*Juniperus communis* only has one line). The branches and leaves are distilled to obtain cade or juniper oil used in veterinary and human medicine to treat different types of dermatitis. According to Palau i Ferrer, the peasants believed that the fruit facilitated expulsion of the placenta and used to dose female livestock with ¼ litre of the extract when expulsion was delayed after birth. According to Guerau d'Arellano, there are numerous uses for the plant in Ibiza: the authentic peasant castanets are made with juniper rootstock; wine barrels are cleaned with water in which juniper splints have been boiled; and pipes and furniture, particularly mirror frames, are made from the wood.

Mediterranean mezereon, *Daphne gnidium* (7), is to be found throughout the islands, but generally in isolated examples. This is a shrub that grows to a height of one metre. Its branches

7. *Daphne gnidium.* Mediterranean mezereon.   8. *Cneorum tricoccon.*

are vertical; its leaves narrow, frequently turned so that they also lie in a vertical plane (see p. 14), are of a light green color that can be clearly seen from a distance. In mid-summer the plant produces groups of small white flowers which last a long time and are later followed by small round red or black fruit. Despite its attractive appearance and the pleasant fragrance of its flowers, it is a fairly poisonous shrub. Its resin contains a bitter-tasting alkaloid, daphnine; the fruit and leaves are a not very recommendable purgative.

Cneorum tricoccon (**8**) is fairly common in drier areas with poorer soil. This little shrub is frequently less than one metre tall. It is easy to recognize with its long upturned leaves (see p. 14). It has small yellow flowers and a highly characteristic fruit with the three "berries" of its scientific name. When half-ripe the fruit is bright red, then finally it turns black. The family

Cneoraceae is curious in that it consists of only one genus with two species — the other is the *Cneorum pulverulentum* of the Canary Islands. Our species is endemic to the western Mediterranean, with a fairly odd, discontinuous distribution as will be seen from Map 3. In the Balearic Islands it is more frequent in the southern area. Thus it abounds in Ibiza, but is rare and highly localized in Minorca.

Another shrub which is curious from a taxonomic viewpoint is the wild joint-pine (*Ephedra fragilis*). Not only is it the sole representative of the family *Ephedraceae* in the Balearic Islands, but it is also the only representative of its order, *Gnetales*. Furthermore, it is a plant of singular appearance: the leaves and flowers are rudimentary and insignificant; all one sees is a fairly dense multitude of vertical branches. These branches are jointed and if we attempt to dry them they come apart completely, thus living up to their botanical name of *fragilis*. This shrub is to be found both in the mountains and by the sea in Majorca. There are lovely examples at Portals Vells just behind the main bay and even more beautiful examples at Cabrera, on the rise leading to the castle.

The joint-pine, which may grow to a small tree with a height of three metres and a good-sized trunk, is not to be confused with a shrub that is very similar in appearance, but never grows taller than one metre or has a real trunk, and which has tiny, but visible, leaves. This is *Osyris alba* (9) which is quite common in the forests of Majorca, but very rare in Minorca. In Ibiza it is replaced by the *Osyris quadripartita*.

The Pea Family

The plant family best represented in the Balearic Islands is that of the peas, or *Leguminosae,* estimated to include 11% of the total number of species. It is a complex family with three subfamilies: the *Caesalpinioideae,* only two species of which are indigenous to Europe: the carob which we have already discussed, and the Judas tree (*Cercis siliquastrum*), sometimes planted as an

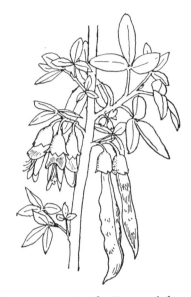

9. *Osyris alba.*   10. *Anagyris foetida.* Bean trefoil.

ornamental tree on some of the island's estates; the *Mimosoideae*,
no species of which is indigenous to Europe, but with many representatives of the *Acacia* genus (erroneously called "mimosas")
introduced as garden trees; and the third, and by far most important family, the *Lotoideae* or *Papilionaceae* with a variety of
species which are economically important (alfalfa, beans, peas,
lentils, clover, not to mention the peanut and soya bean).

One of the most ancient representatives of this last sub-
family is the bean trefoil (*Anagyris foetida*) (**10**). This is a shrub
which can grow up to three metres tall, with large trifoliate leaves
which seem improbable in a plant of this size. The yellow
flowers, which bloom in winter, are always found in the inner
part of the shrub, never on the tips of the branches. The fruit
is a large, somewhat flattened bean. The scientific name comes
from the unpleasant smell the plant gives off — a warning of
its poisonous nature. But in limited quantities it is used in me-

dicine: the leaves as a purgative and the seed (which contain
the alkaloid, anagyrine) as an emetic. Although never abundan
in the Islands it is found here and there (there are a fair numbe
of these plants near Bellver Castle).

The thorny broom (*Calicotome spinosa*) is the same size, bu
much more common (**11**). It is well known for its impressiv
thorns 4-5 cms long. This is a plant that varies greatly accordin
to the season. In winter it is green with small trifoliate leave
In spring it bursts into bloom with a really glorious mass o
yellow flowers. In summer the fruit and sometimes the leave
turn black before falling (see p. 12).

Although the thorny broom is a plant limited to the wester
Mediterranean, it has a relative, quite similar in appearance
which is endemic to Majorca: *Genista lucida* (**12**). It is difficul
to distinguish the flowers and form of the two species. Howeve
Genista lucida is usually lower and thicker, with narrower, mor
graceful branches and thorns. But the best way to tell then
apart is by the leaves: *Genista lucida* has very small, simpl

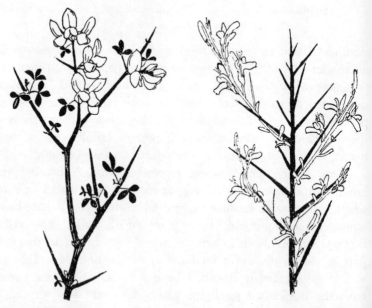

11. *Calicotome spinosa*. Thorny broom.   12. *Genista lucida*.

'not trifoliate) leaves, and very few of them or sometimes even none at all. Furthermore, it usually blooms earlier in March, whereas thorny broom flowers in April, but this is a rule with many exceptions. *Genista lucida* is localized in the eastern part of Majorca between Randa and Artà and in the western corner between Galilea, Sant Telm and Santa Ponça. A good place to compare the two species is the pass to Galilea, on the road which comes up from Puigpunyent. *Genista lucida* does not exist in the other Balearic Islands.

A leguminous plant typical of dry, sun-baked lands is *Anthyllis cytisoides* (**13**), a little shrub with vertical branches and small leaves (simple or trifoliate) which fall in the summer (see p. 12). This plant, which seldom reaches one metre in height, is easy to recognize as it is all of a silvery hue, except for its yellow flowers. Outside the western Balearic Islands (it is rare or non-existent in Minorca), this plant is only to be found in the south of France, the south and east of Spain, Morocco and Algeria.

13.   *Anthyllis cytisoides.*
14.   *Globularia alypum.* Shrubby globularia.
15.   *Rosmarinus officinalis.* Rosemary.

In the old days its smooth flexible branches were used to make the frames employed in raising silk worms.

Associated with this plant, we frequently find the shrubby globularia, *Globularia alypum* (**14**), of the family *Globulariaceae,* which has small pointed, leathery leaves and a pale blue inflorescence. We use the technical word here because if we take apart what appears to be a flower, we find that in reality it consists of a head of tiny flowers, each one entire and complete. And this inflorescence blooms almost all year long, but mainly in the autumn.

The Mint and Rockrose Families

Another family which is of economic importance in the Mediterranean is the mint family or *Labiatae,* whose essential oils provide fragrances for perfumes and for cooking (mint, lavender, sage, marjoram, oregano, etc.). Its best known representative is almost certainly rosemary, *Rosmarinus officinalis* (**15**) (see Map 5) with its inrolled leaves like those of heather (see pp. 14 and 25) and with its sky blue (and, more infrequently, white or even pink) flowers which bloom almost all year round.

It is a many-faceted plant: aesthetic (as a border species in gardens), culinary (simply crush a couple of leaves between your fingers to savor its delicious fragrance), medicinal; it is important in the production of honey (the flowers have abundant nectar) and it is employed in perfume making. As we can see from a one-act play of the 17th century,[5] rosemary was formerly used as incense:

> "Any merchant or barberer of wigs
> burns his small rosemary springs
> And among the ladies schooled in vice
> Rosemary's burnt, or 'tis not so nice.
> In short, my beloved mother often said
> That from this smoke the devil fled".

---

[5] *La casa de juego* by Francisco Navarrete.

In Greek and Roman times crowns were made of rosemary for public celebrations and religious ceremonies; in the Middle Ages it was an important ingredient in love potions and all sorts of elixirs. So it may be said that there is no aspect of human life in which rosemary has not played a role. It is found more or less everywhere in the Balearic Islands, growing from sea level to the highest mountains, where one finds the endemic variety *palaui* which is lower, more straggling and gnarled.[6]

The two local species of lavender are oddly distributed in our islands. The *Lavandula stoechas* or French lavender (**17**), common throughout the Mediterranean and used in the perfume industry in France, is to be found only in Minorca and Ibiza.

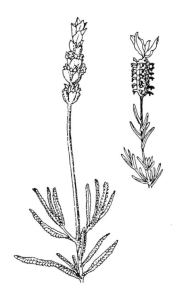

However, the toothed lavender or *Lavandula dentata* (**16**), which is an Ibero-Mauritanian species, is found only in Majorca and in Ibiza. The two plants are easy to tell apart, the leaves of the latter having their margins cut into rounded teeth, as its scientific name implies. The inflorescence of the genus is also odd. Atop a long peduncle a dense spike is formed mainly by violet-coloured bracts (leaves associated with inflorescences), which many people think are the flowers themselves. But a closer look reveals that the true flowers are small, whitish in colour and half-hidden among these bracts.

The rockrose family is well represented in the oak woods of

16. *Lavandula dentata.*
     Toothed lavender.
17. *Lavandula stoechas.*
     French lavender.

---

[6] This v. *palaui* has now been found also on the coasts of Majorca and Minorca, but not Ibiza, where similar exposure to wind does not seem to cause the same deformation.

the Balearic Islands, by species belonging to the genus *Cistus*.
The best known and easiest to identify is the *Cistus albidus* or
grey-leaved cistus (**18**) with its greyish leaves and pink flowers.
The plant is found only in the western Mediterranean (see Map 6).
Equally common here is *Cistus monspeliensis* (**19**), the narrow-
leaved cistus with its slender, lanceshaped leaves and white
flowers which are smaller than those of the other four species.

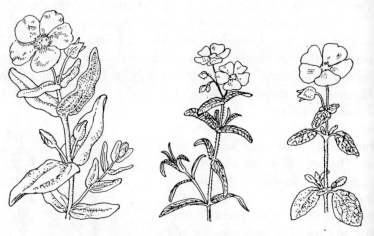

18. *Cistus albidus.* Grey-leaved cistus.
19. *Cistus monspeliensis.* Narrow-leaved cistus.
20. *Cistus salvifolius.* Sage-leaved cistus.

The leaves are somewhat viscous to the touch and give off a delicious resiny fragrance, especially in the hottest part of the summer when the plant perfumes the entire forest. It was probably
that fragrance which caused Napoleon to say: "Les yeux fermés,
à l'odeur seule, je reconnaîtrais ma Corse". This species is somewhat more amply distributed than the former (see Map 6). The
third common species (but not as common as the other two) is
the sage-leaved cistus *Cistus salvifolius* (**20**), with soft oval leaves
and an attractive white flower about the same size as that of the
Cistus albidus (see also Map 6).

There are two rarer cistuses in the Balearic Islands. One of
them is *Cistus clusii* of Ibiza and Formentera which is found in

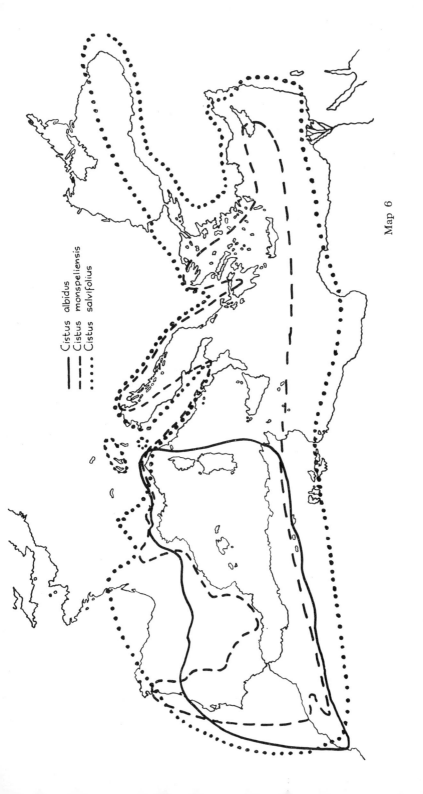

Cistus albidus
Cistus monspeliensis
Cistus salvifolius

Map 6

Majorca in only limited quantities on the southern dunes from
Porto Pi to Cape Salines. It resembles *Cistus monspeliensis,* but
its leaves are still narrower (1-2 mm wide while the leaves of the
monspeliensis are 4-8 mm wide). It is an Ibero-Mauritanian species
which is also found in Sicily and Calabria. The other rare rockrose
is *Cistus incanus* or *villosus* of Minorca which is found in Majorca
only in a small area of the dunes between the Albufera of Alcúdia
and the sea. It is very similar to *Cistus albidus,* from which it
can be distinguished by a detail of the leaves: the leaves of *Cistus
albidus* arise directly from the branches while the leaves of this
rarer plant have 3-15 mm stalks. It is an eastern Mediterranean
species and the Balearic Islands are its westernmost point of
growth (it is completely absent from mainland France and the
Iberian Peninsula).

We cannot leave cistuses without mentioning two very
strange plants which live parasitically on their roots: *Cytinus
ruber* (the most common) which lives off pink flowered cistus,
and *Cytinus hypocistis* which lives off the white flowered species.
They have no leaves (nor do they need them, given their para-
sitical nature); all that is visible above the earth's surface are the
fleshy flowers which are reddish orange on the outside and
yellowish white inside. At the base of the flowers there is a
sweet juice, like a bland honey, which children like to suck.

The Lily Family; Vines

The lily family, or *Liliaceae,* is also important in the Balearic Islands. This family has such a variety of forms that
many botanists divide it into four subfamilies: the *Colchiceae*
(of which the only representative in the Islands is *Merendera
filifolia* which we will discuss in the section on mountain plants
(see p. 87); the *Dracaenoideae,* named for the famous *Dracaena
draco* of the Canary Islands, which exists here only as a cultivated species — the yucca; the *Asphodeloideae,* the most important of the sub-families, which includes the asphodel themselves as well as onions, garlic, grape hyacinth, lilies, etc., and

finally the *Asparagoideae,* which includes butcher's broom, asparagus and sarsaparilla, which we will now discuss.

Ruscus aculeatus (**21**) has several common names. While in English the entire plant is called butcher's broom, the Majorcans have a separate name for the red fruit which blooms so attractively in the center of the leaf. It is called the little cherry of Bethlehem or of the Good Shepherd and is used as a Christmas decoration. By using the word "leaf" in reference to this plant, however, we have fallen into a common error. All we need do is to observe that first the little white flower and later the fruit sprout in the middle of this organ to realize that it could never be a leaf. Indeed, it is a modified branch — flattened out and equipped with the plant's photosynthetic mechanism — which scientists call a cladode. The true leaf is reduced to a long scale which resembles a stipule situated beneath the cladode. It should also be recalled that these cladodes are tilted vertically upwards in order to reduce transpiration (see p. 14).

Loss of leaf is total in the genus *Asparagus,* of which there are three species in the Balearic Islands (not counting the cultivated *Asparagus officinalis* and other decorative garden plants). The most important is the *Asparagus stipularis* (**22**) with its cla-

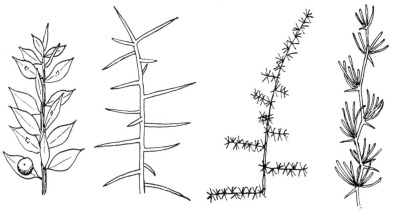

21. *Ruscus aculeatus.* Butcher's broom.
22. *Asparagus stipularis.*
23. *Asparagus acutifolius.*
24. *Asparagus albus.*

dode transformed into sharp thorns measuring 2-3 cm in length. However, the tender shoots, which sprout in spring, make excellent eating. This is a southern European species, absent, for example, from France, Corsica or Italy. In *Asparagus acutifolius* (**23**), the cladodes are bunched in groups of 4-12, but they are still stiff and pointed. This species occurs throughout the entire Mediterranean. The morphology of *Asparagus albus* (**24**) is somewhat more complicated. The length of the cladodes is midway between that of the other two species (10-20 mm.), but they are soft and deciduous. They grow in bunches like those of the *acutifolius*, but here we find in each group a leaf or scale transformed into a quite hard, pointed thorn measuring 5-10 mm in length. Usually both this thorn and the stem of the plant are white when mature, thus giving the plant its name of *albus*. The species is found only in the western Mediterranean, excluding France and the north of Italy.

25. *Smilax aspera* v. *balearica*.
26. *Smilax aspera*. European sarsaparilla.

The other member of this sub-family is the European sarsaparilla or *Smilax aspera* (**26**). Here we will not find cladodes, but we do find truly surprising variations in the size of the leaves, which grow quite large in cool, shady places or in rich soil and are small and narrow when the plant grows in places greatly exposed to the sun. This latter is the var. *balearica* (**25**), endemic to our islands. In the mountains (as well as Cape Blanc) it sometimes even takes the shape of a little cushion without a single leaf. This species is well-known to hikers for its backward curving thorns (sometimes hidden beneath the leaf) which catch on clothing. It should be mentioned that the tender shoots are edible, as are those of all the species of this sub-family, although the *Asparagus stipularis* is the most appreciated of all of them.

Sarsaparilla serves as an introduction to the climbers and scramblers of the woods. Probably the best known and most feared for its thorns (which also curve backwards) is the bramble (*Rubus ulmifolius*) (**27**). This may climb over large expanses of wall or quite simply rise up independently to erect a solid barrier on the banks of streams or elsewhere. No matter how annoying the bramble may be to the hiker, it has its good points too. It's a wonderful refuge for small birds like warblers, which can safely build their nests there; it has medicinal properties — Palau says that throat and mouth inflammations and hoarseness can be cured by chewing the young, still tender sprouts. Furthermore, the blackberries are edible and make excellent jams and jellies.

From the same family of *Rosaceae* comes the wild rose — *Rosa sempervirens* (**28**) — which also grows up walls and climbs

27. *Rubus ulmifolius*. Bramble.
28. *Rosa sempervirens*. Wild rose.

up shrubs. The flower, with its five simple white petals, bears little resemblance to domestic roses, the product of centuries of carefully studied deformation.

Another species with curved thorns is the wild madder, but here the thorns are microscopic. They can only be seen through a good magnifying glass or noted by brushing a finger or a piece of cloth across the underside of a leaf and seeing how it catches there. The leaves are clustered in groups of 4 or 6, with quadrangular stems. The common species throughout not only the Balearic Islands but the entire Mediterranean is the *Rubia peregrina* (**29**). But in Majorca there is also an endemic species — *Rubia angustifolia* — with smaller, narrower leaves.

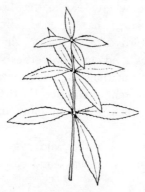

29.   *Rubia peregrina.*

The most beautiful forest climber is surely the *Lonicera implexa,* or honeysuckle (**30**), which takes its name from the fact that the base of the flower is filled with a nectar which children are fond of. Furthermore, the flower gives off an exquisite fragrance, particularly at night. The plant is easily distinguishable by its upper leaves which are joined in pairs and have a fine transparent margin.

Two other forest climbers belong to the genus *Clematis.* Each one blooms in a different season and when few other plants are in flower. In mid-summer, when almost all vegetation is scorched by the sun, we can be certain that the white cloud we see blooming on a fence, in a forest or hedge is *Clematis flammula* or fragrant clematis (**31**). The leaves are so sharply dissected that the leaflets look like separate leaves. The plant also appears to bloom for a long time, but what actually happens is that once the blossom dies a long, hairy style sprouts. When seen from a distance, it gives the same cloud-like impression as the flowers. The plant's Latin name comes from the caustic, blistering properties which give the leaves the taste of a "little flame". Palau says

30.   *Lonicera implexa.* Honeysuckle.
31.   *Clematis flammula.* Fragrant clematis.

that its French name, *herbe aux gueux* (beggar's weed) comes
from its having been used by certain beggars to produce sores
designed to arouse pity. The plant is common only in Majorca. In
Minorca it is restricted to the coastal dunes and cooler places in
the interior; in Ibiza it is extremely rare.

The other species, *Clematis cirrhosa* or virgin's bower (**32**)
blooms in the middle of winter. It also differs from *Clematis flammula* in that it grows in abundance on all the Balearic Islands
and at any altitude, from sea level at S'Arenal to the peaks of
Puig Major and Maçanella (where it naturally blooms later: in
the spring or at the beginning of summer). It is like the *flammula*
species only in that once the flower has died, a very long, hairy
pistil appears. Furthermore, it is an extremely variable species:
the long drooping bell-shaped flower is usually white with violet
spots on the inside, but it may occur without spots (i.e. completely
white) or it may be so closely spotted as to appear quite dark in
color. However, it is the leaf that reveals the most amazing variations: it may be simple, it may be more or less deeply lobed

or it may be incised to such an extent that there are completely separate leaflets, each one with its own little stem. The latter is var. *balearica* which, despite its name, is also found in Corsica, Sardinia and North Africa.

A climber as well known as ivy (*Hedera helix*) needs no description. We have all seen it growing on cliffs, climbing up

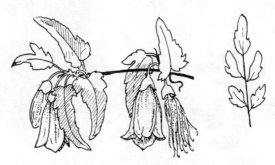

32. *Clematis cirrhosa*. Virgin's bower.

trees, and covering country cottages. In the Balearics it even grows in the highest mountains, where I have seen it growing on rock-faces, with the first metre and a half as completely bare of leaves as if it had been trimmed by a gardener. The "gardener" in this case are the sheep who are particularly fond of ivy leaves. As an item of curiosity, the reader will note that the plant has two forms — one which it takes when it finds support against a wall, tree, etc. and another when that support comes to an end. It then no longer has adhesive rootlets, the leaves have no lobes, and the plant produces flowers and fruit (which, in the preceding form, it is incapable of doing). Furthermore, by planting a cutting of this latter form we can produce a straightgrowing shrub (a trick employed in landscape gardening).

We cannot leave climbers without mentioning black bryony (*Tamus communis*), not because it is so common (it is found only in cool places), but because the beginner may confuse it with the young sarsaparilla. It has similar, heart-shaped leaves, but they are softer and have no thorns.

Smaller Plants: Other Members of the Lily Family and the Arum Family

There are so many smaller plants in the woods that we will have to deal with them rather briefly and choosing only the most notable of them. Probably the best known are the two species of asphodel (of the *Liliaceae* family, sub-family *Asphodeloideae,* see p. 40) which we have in the Balearic Islands: *Asphodelus aestivus* (= *A. microcarpus*) (**33**) and *Asphodelus fistulosus* (**34**).[7]

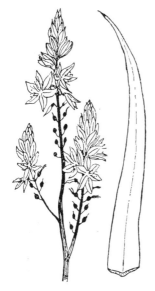

33. *Asphodelus aestivus.*   34. *Asphodelus fistulosus.*

The former is considerably taller, but differs primarily in the shape of its leaf. The leaves of *aestivus* have v-shaped sections while those of *fistulosus* have hollow circular sections (see illustration).

---

[7] A third, *Asphodelus albus,* was recently discovered in Ibiza, on the Penyal d'Eivissa.

The asphodel is a plant that may be found anywhere, though its preference is for fallow, over-grazed ground. This may possibly be the reason the Greeks associated it with the dead: they planted it on graves and, according to them, the underground kingdom of souls was carpeted with them (Homer's famous "fields of asphodels"). More recently, the tubers, rich in starch, were used to make the glue employed by shoemakers and bookbinders.

One of the wild plants which most resembles a garden species is the gladiolus. Here the commonest species is the *Gladiolus illyricus*, but *G. italicus* (= *G. segetum*) is also to be found, as is *G. communis*, recently discovered in Puigpunyent. It is difficult to distinguish between them. They all have sword-like leaves and a spike of lovely flowers, which all face in the same direction.

Possibly the oddest looking plant family to be found in the Balearic Islands is that of the *Araceae*, represented here by the friar's cowl, *Arisarum vulgare* (**35**), two plants of the genus *Arum* — *A. italicum* or Italian arum (**36**), *A. pictum* or painted arum, and *Dracunculus muscivorus* (= *Arum muscivorum*). The inflorescence of all of them consists of a central column (the spadix) surrounded by a type of sheath (the spathe). In *Arisarum* this sheath forms a sort of tube which permits only the tip of the spadix to emerge; in *Arum* the spathe is straight and closed only at the base. *Arum italicum*, more common by far, is abundant in non-cultivated fields — the spadix and spathe are yellow. *Arum pictum* — a Tyrrhenian species abundant in the mountains of Majorca and the coastal zones of Llucmajor and rarer elsewhere — has a purple spadix and spathe. *Dracunculus muscivorus* — another Tyrrhenian species, but much less common in the Balearic Islands, being limited almost exclusively to some parts of the Majorcan mountains, Minorca and Cabrera — also has a purple spadix and spathe, but they are spotted and the leaves of the plant are incised in a very odd way. The scientific name of this latter plant comes from the fact that, like all arums, it traps flies at the base of the spadix. Formerly it was believed that the plants ate the insects, but now we know that this has to do with pollinization, by means of one of nature's most extraor-

linary processes. When the female flowers, which are grouped
at the base of the spadix, are mature and ready to be pollina-
ed, the inflorescence begins to give off a fetid odour, accompanied by a rise in temperature. The smell and the heat attract
lies covered with pollen from other plants. They descend into
he spathe where they are trapped by the sticky walls and by a
eries of hairs located halfway up the spadix which prevent them
rom getting out. In their struggle to escape, the flies dust female
lowers with the pollen they are carrying. Then, when night falls,
he plant undergoes a complicated transformation. The female
lowers wilt and the male flowers (located somewhat higher up)
begin showering their pollen on the trapped insects and, at the
same time, the temperature drops and the fetid odour vanishes.
By the following morning the walls are less sticky and the barri-
cading hairs have wilted, leaving the flies free to visit other
plants with their new loads of pollen.

Without the inflorescence, the leaves of the arum could be
confused with those of *Cyclamen balearicum* (**37**). The leaves of
the cyclamen are greyish in colour, mottled and usually smaller

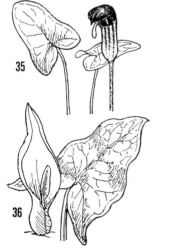
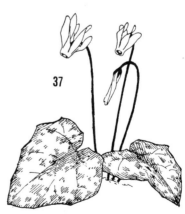

35. *Arisarum vulgare.* Friar's cowl.
36. *Arum italicum.* Italian arum.
37. *Cyclamen balearicum.*

than those of the arum. But the cyclamen's flower differs totally from that of the arum; it is small, white and drooping, with turned-up petals. Apart from the Balearic Islands this species is found only in the Fenouillèdes district in the south of France and thus may be said to be quasi-endemic.

The Orchid and Spurge Families

Almost as strange as that of the arums is the pollinization process of the orchids, a family which is well represented in the Balearic Islands as it is throughout the Mediterranean. Naturally, they are not those spectacular orchids which grow on jungle trees and are cultivated in greenhouses: ours grow in the earth and are quite small, but that does not prevent them from being beautiful, interesting, and from sometimes even having strange and exotic forms.

The most common genus is *Ophrys* which is recognizable by the flower's disproportionately large and inflated lower lip, which is frequently furry or velvety-textured. The most common of them all is *Ophrys fusca* or brown bee orchid (**44**), which begins blooming in January. The upper part of its lip is metallic blue and the lower part almost black, terminating in four lobes. *Ophrys bertolonii* (**43**) has a completely black, velvety lip marked by a single light spot in the center. *Ophrys sphegodes*, or early spider orchid, represented by the sub-species *atrata* (**42**) here, has two bags or lateral "shoulders" and a center spot which, though variable, is usually in the shape of an H. Almost as common as the first-named species, is the well-known mirror orchid or mirror-of-Venus, *Ophrys speculum* (**39**), which has a hairy-edged lip with a shiny centre which has given it its name. The smallest and most oddly-shaped of the orchids is *Ophrys bombyliflora* or bumble-bee orchid (**41**), whose tiny, furry flower with two side "arms" like stubby wings more than justifies its name. The two most eye-catching species are surely *Ophrys tenthredinifera* or sawfly orchid (**40**) and *Ophrys apifera* or bee orchid (**38**). Both of them have three pink back petals (which are actually sepals): bright

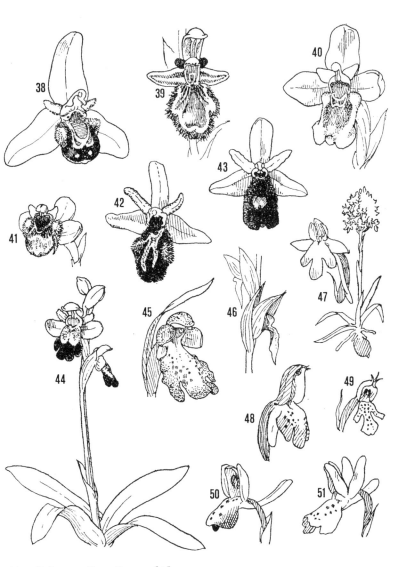

38. *Ophrys apifera*. Bee orchid.
39.   „   *speculum*. Mirror orchid, mirror-of-Venus.
40.   „   *tenthredinifera*. Sawfly orchid.
41.   „   *bombyliflora*. Bumble-bee orchid.
42.   „   *sphegodes* ssp. *atrata*. Early spider orchid.
43.   „   *bertolonii*.
44.   „   *fusca*. Brown bee orchid.
45. *Barlia robertiana*.
46. *Serapias lingua*. Tongue orchid.
47. *Anacamptis pyramidalis*. Pyramidal orchid.
48. *Orchis coriophora*. Bug orchid.
49.   „   *tridentata*. Toothed orchid.
50.   „   *longicornu*. Long-spurred orchid.
51.   „   *mascula*. Early purple orchid.

pink in the case of the former and paler, whitish pink in the latter. *Ophrys tenthredinifera* has a squarer, hairy lip with a hook-shaped protuberance at the tip, while *Ophrys apifera* has a rounder, shiny lip, only the two little side pouches of which are hairy. The only species of this genus which is not illustrated here is *Ophrys lutea*, which is rare in Majorca and Ibiza (but less so in Minorca). It is easily identifiable by its very wide lip with a bright yellow margin which is as wide as the blue and brown centre.

This is the genus which has such a curious pollinization process. Certain male bees, attracted by the shape of the lip and particularly by its characteristic odour are led to believe that it is a female of their species. They mount the lip and begin copulating. Their position is such that they cannot avoid contact with the pollinia (two pouches of pollen in the shape of rigid clubs with sticky bases which cause the pouches to stick to the insect's body — usually its head) so that when the bee flies away it takes the pouches with it. Then an extraordinary hygroscopic movement begins: the pollinia, hitherto vertical, begin to bend and after a quarter or half a minute they are almost completely horizontal, in a perfect position to touch the stigma of the next orchid visited by the bee as it makes its rounds.

The other genus which is fairly frequent in the Mediterranean is *Orchis*. To my way of thinking, this includes the two most beautiful orchids of our islands, *Orchis longicornu* or long-spurred orchid (**50**), and *Orchis mascula* or early purple orchid (**51**). The former has the sepals and petals united in a sort of helmet, while the two side sepals of the latter are bent back, giving the flower a more open appearance. But both have an extremely long spur, a lip with the sides bending downward, and a truly amazing variety of color. They range from almost completely white to dramatic mixtures of red, purple and black. The former has been found in a few places in Minorca and in the coastal region of Llucmajor in Majorca, but as a rule both of them are found only in the mountains of Majorca. *Orchis coriophora* or bug orchid (**48**) is very different, with its long, compact floral spike, as is *Orchis tridentata* or toothed orchid (**49**), which is small and has its flowers clustered in a thick, conical mass. This latter somewhat resembles *Anacamptis pyrami-dalis* or pyramidal orchid (**47**), which is taller, without purplish spots on the tip, and generally later blooming. Probably our largest orchid,[8] and certainly the one with the greatest number of scientific synonyms, is *Barlia robertiana,* which until recently was called *Himantoglossum* (or *Loroglossum, Aceras* or *Orchis*) *longibracteatum* (**45**). It usually starts blooming early (around the month of February) and, I don't quite know why, but it has an unhealthy appearance, as though it were a carnivorous or poisonous plant — which it is not.

Very different in shape is the genus *Serapias,* with *Serapias lingua* or tongue orchid (**46**), and *Serapias parviflora* or small-flowered serapias, which are rather hard to tell apart. The first, more common in Majorca and Minorca, but unknown in Ibiza, has a larger hood which juts forward; the second, rarer in Majorca and Minorca, but very common in Ibiza and Formentera, has a smaller hood which tilts slightly backward. But variations in shape, and the fact that one never sees them together, makes it difficult to apply these criteria of identification. The best way to distinguish them is by taking apart a flower in order to look at the base of the lip which is hidden inside. *Serapias lingua* has one hump or protuberance there while *parviflora* has two parallel humps. Similar to these two species is *Limodorum abortivum* which does not have green leaves (because it does not need them to undergo the photosynthesis process as it gets its nourishment directly from decomposing organic material, i.e. to put it scientifically, it is a saprophytic plant). This is a tall, straight orchid, entirely violet except for a touch of yellow in the flower. I have always seen it in fairly shady woods.

This is by no means the end of the list of Balearic orchids, but the others are either rare, localized, or so insignificant in appearance that there is little likelihood of the reader encountering them by chance.

---

8   This is really only the largest of the common orchids. The largest of them is the rare and magnificent *Orchis laxiflora* ssp. *palustris* (which grows to a height of one metre), discovered by Antoni and Lleonard Llorens several years ago in a corner of the Albufera of Alcúdia.

The strangest sort of inflorescence to be found in these islands is certainly that of the genus *Euphorbia* (spurge). These plants have neither petals nor sepals nor do they bear any resemblance to anything which is usually believed to constitute a flower. They have a cup bordered by four glands (sometimes with horns or in the shape of a new moon), from which emerge what appear to be pistil and stamens, but which in reality are a single entire female flower and several entire male flowers. Unfortunately it is a complex genus, with some twenty species in the Balearic Islands, all of which are difficult to tell apart. The only two which are easy to identify are the largest ones: *Euphorbia dendroides* (tree spurge), a bush which grows to a height of one and sometimes two metres and is almost always perfectly hemispherical in shape; and the *Euphorbia characias* which, although it may reach a height of a metre and a half, is never as wide or hemispherical as the former. Furthermore the latter may be distinguished by its glands (at the edge of the floral cup) which are reddish brown or black, rather than yellow as in other species. While this spurge is found fairly well everywhere (although it is rare in Ibiza and the south of Majorca), the former prefers the coasts of Santanyí and of the northwestern mountains of Majorca. The plants of this genus contain a milky, poisonous juice (latex). And it is the latex from another plant of the same family (*Hevea brasiliensis*) which gives us rubber.

Other Members of the Pea and Mint Families

There are many interesting smaller plants within the sub-family *Papilionaceae* of the pea family (see p. 32) which grow in the oak forests. The most interesting from a botanical viewpoint is the endemic *Lotus tetraphyllus* (**52**), a small, delicate plant with a tiny yellow flower and a leaf divided into four leaflets as implied by its name. This plant is found only in Majorca and Minorca, almost always (with some exceptions in Minorca) in fairly shady forests. *Dorycnium pentaphyllum* (**53**) with its tiny, narrow leaves consisting of five leaflets (also as indicated by its scientific name) and its diminutive flowers (4-6 mm. long) clustered in close groups of 5 to 15, is fairly common. This plant is second only to rosemary in its importance in the production of honey. Here and there throughout the woods we can find *Dorycnium hirsutum* which is somewhat similar in appearance, but with much larger,

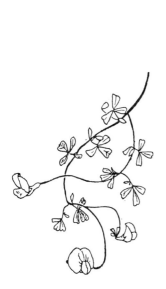

52. *Lotus tetraphyllus.*

53. *Dorycnium pentaphyllum.*

and rather hairy leaves and flowers. We can also find *Psoralea bituminosa* (**54**) with its large leaves divided into three leaflets and its light violet floral heads. This plant is popularly known as pitch trefoil. Both its common and scientific names derive from the fact that the crushed leaf gives off a strong smell — almost unbelievable in a plant — of tar. Although many people find the smell disagreeable, I find it more surprising than unpleasant.

Of the mint family (see p. 36) we can find three species of germander, *Teucrium*, which are immediately recognizable by their lavender flowers which have no upper lip or "helmet" (this genus is also important in the high mountains (see p. 82 and 83). The first is *Teucrium chamaedrys* (wall germander) with opposite, dentate leaves which vaguely resemble those of an oak. The other two, *Teucrium capitatum* and *T. polium*, are difficult to tell apart, but both have such a hairy stem and leaves that they are almost white, and they have little flowers grouped in compact heads.

54. *Psoralea bituminosa*. Pitch trefoil.   55. *Teucrium polium*.

The Daisy and Other Families

An important, but often difficult, family for the beginner is the *Compositae* or daisy family, which we know from a multitude of cultivated plants (artichoke, lettuce, sunflower, chamomile, zinnia, dahlia, field marigold, etc.). When what seems to be a flower is taken apart we discovered that, as in the *Globulariaceae*, it is really a cluster of tiny flowers growing very close to one another. Each has an ovary (which will be the fruit) above which there is the corolla (the petals as a group), frequently surrounded by a crown of long white hairs which unfold like a silky parachute when the fruit is ripe and leave the wind to do the job of spreading the seeds. The corolla may be tubular or tongue-shaped; those *Compositae* which have tubular flowers at least in the centre disc comprise the sub-family of the *Tubuliflorae*.

Those which consist entirely of tongue-shaped flowers (and a milky juice in the plant) constitute the sub-family of the *Liguliflorae*. In this family the head of the flower is surrounded by an involucre of bracts and supported by a receptacle (in the artichoke the part we eat is this receptacle — the "heart" — and the fleshy base of the bracts).

A good example of the *Tubuliflorae* are the three species of daisies which we find in the woods. All three have yellow, tubular-shaped flowers in the centre d'sc, and tongue-shaped, white (often somewhat purplish underneath) flowers around the edge. The species which blooms in October and November and only has leaves at its base is *Bellis sylvestris* or southern daisy (**56**). A smaller species which blooms in spring (although it sometimes is already blooming by Christmas) is *Bellis annua* or annual daisy (**57**), with leaves on the stem as well as at the base. The smallest species (the head of flowers is 6-15 mm. in diameter and the plant is 3-15 cm. tall) is *Bellium bellidioides* (**58**), most frequently to be found in the mountains. Like the first mentioned of these

56.   *Bellis sylvestris.* Southern daisy.
57.   *Bellis annua.* Annual daisy.
58.   *Bellium bellidioides.*

species, all its leaves are at the base of the plant with petioles that are filiform, like the stem itself. This plant is a Tyrrhenian endemic, i.e. it is to be found only in the Balearic Islands, Corsica and Sardinia.

One of the *Compositae* which every Majorcan knows, or has felt scratching his ankles, as he rambled though the countryside, is the flat-topped carline thistle, *Carlina corymbosa* (**59**), of which

59. *Carlina corymbosa*. Flat-topped carline thistle.
60. *Scabiosa atropurpurea*. Mournful widow, sweet scabious.

the Balearic Islands have the endemic sub-species *involucrata*. Like all thistles it is a member of the sub-family of the *Tubuliflorae*, but has no tongue-shaped flowers. It is an exceedingly spiny biennial. By the time its yellow flowers bloom in the summer the rest of the plant appears dry and half-dead. It is surely the most abundant of Balearic thistles (see p. 66 for others), and can be found anywhere from the plains to the mountain peaks.

There are three plants which often fool the beginner because they look like *compositae* but aren't. The first of them is *Eryngium campestre* or field eryngo, which, like its dune-growing brother, the sea holly (see p. 115), is not a thistle at all, but an umbellifer, with its umbel or parasol of little flowers grouped in the shape of a ball. Its Majorcan name "card girgoler" or mushroom thistle comes from the fact that old specimens of the plant are sometimes host to a parasitic mushroom *Pleurotus eryngii* which is very good to eat.

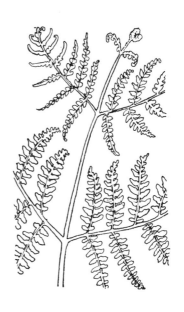

The second of these deceptive plants is the *Globularia* which we have previously described (p. 36). The third is the mournful widow or sweet scabious, *Scabiosa atropurpurea* (= *S. maritima*) (**60**), which has larger lateral flowers, giving the inflorescence a slightly flattened appearance, and opposite leaves which are cleft in a very characteristic way. These last two species belong, respectively, to the *Globulariaceae* and the *Dipsacaceae* families, and may be told apart (and from the *Compositae*) by details of the flowers.

61. *Pteridium aquilinum.*
Bracken.

The most noteworthy member of the grass family (see p. 72) in the Balearics is doubtless *Ampelodesmos mauritanica** (= *A. tenax*), which is very common throughout Majorca and Minorca, growing anywhere from beside the sea to the highest mountain peaks. On the other hand, it is more localized on Ibiza, and on Cabrera it exists in only one spot, a fact which is odd considering the largely North African distribution of the plant (see map 3). In Majorca it keeps the mountainsides green even in summer, which is very rare in a climate like that of the Mediterranean. *Ampelodesmos* was traditionally used to make the roofing over charcoal burners' huts, and the tender leaves as animal fodder.

Bracken (*Pteridium aquilinum*) (**61**) is a fern that is fairly common in the mountains of Majorca, extremely rare in Minorca and non-existent in the other islands. It is not a higher plant in the sense of having flowers and seeds. Like all the members of its order the *Filicopsida*, it reproduces by means of spores developed on the underside of the leaves. Unlike *Ampelodesmos mauretanica*, it is one of our most cosmopolitan plants: it is found in America, Asia, Africa, Australasia, and throughout Europe.

Communities of Woodlands and Scrub

Now that we have some idea of the most common plants of the Balearic forests, it would be a good idea to organize our knowledge, grouping the plants according to their natural communities, providing ourselves with a more accurate picture of the landscape. In order to do this we must know something about the classification system used by botanists. They distinguish four categories of communities which, with their endings and with examples taken from the oak forests of the Balearic Islands, are:

Class	— *etea*	*Quercetea ilicis*
Order	— *etalia*	*Quercetalia ilicis*
Alliance	— *ion*	*Quercion ilicis*
Association	— *etum*	*Cyclamini-Quercetum ilicis*

Here we will ignore the first as it is too general to help us in classifying our ideas. Neither will we go into the details and complications of the last one for the time being. As far as alliances are concerned, there are three main ones within our oak forest, two of which belong to the same order. They can be schematically represented as follows:

Order: *Quercetalia ilicis*   *Rosmarinetalia*

Alliance: *Quercion ilicis*   *Oleo-Ceratonion*   *Rosmarino-Ericion*

The most typical plants of the *Quercion ilicis* are:

Quercus ilex (holm oak)
Arbutus unedo (strawberry tree)
Lonicera implexa (honeysuckle)
Asparagus acutifolius
Ruscus aculeatus (butcher's broom)
Euphorbia characias (spurge)
Daphne gnidium (Mediterranean mezereon)
Teucrium chamaedrys (wall germander)
Phillyrea latifolia
Rhamnus ludovici-salvatoris
Erica arborea (tree heather)

This does not mean that every square metre of oak forest must have these eleven plants or that they will be found there in equal quantity. Quite the contrary. Some of them (like *Phillyrea latifolia*) are fairly rare in the Balearic forests and others are rather highly localized (like *Rhamnus ludovici-salvatoris* and tree heather). But in any part of the true oak forest we will find the majority of these plants. In any case, if we find a part of the forest where these plants —or at least a good number of them— are dominant, we will know that we are in the *Quercion ilicis*.

The most typical plants of the *Oleo-Ceratonion* are:

Olea europaea v. *silvestris* (wild olive)
Ceratonia siliqua (carob)
Clematis cirrhosa (virgin's bower)
Asparagus albus
Asparagus stipularis
Cneorum tricoccon
Chamaerops humilis (dwarf fan palm)
Euphorbia dendroides (tree spurge)
Ephedra fragilis (joint-pine)
Arum pictum (painted arum)

The three (or even four) last-named plants are quite localized, so the fact that they are not present does not mean that we are not in an area of *Oleo-Ceratonion*.

Now there are certain plants which are characteristic of the order *Quercetalia ilicis,* and thus we may find them in either of the two aforementioned alliances. They are:

>*Pistacia lentiscus* (mastic tree or lentisk)
>*Rhamnus alaternus* (Mediterranean buckthorn)
>*Phillyrea angustifolia*
>*Rubia peregrina* (wild madder)
>*Clematis flammula* (fragrant clematis)
>*Cyclamen balearicum*

The third important alliance —the *Rosmarino-Ericion*— includes the following characteristic plants:

>*Erica multiflora*
>*Anthyllis cytisoides*
>*Globularia alypum*
>*Lavandula dentata* (toothed lavender)
>*Rosmarinus officinalis* (rosemary)
>*Genista lucida*
>*Teucrium polium*
>*Gladiolus illyricus*
>*Ophrys tenthredinifera* (sawfly orchid)
>*Ophrys speculum* (mirror orchid)
>*Ophrys bombyliflora* (bumblebee orchid)
>*Anacamptis pyramidalis* (pyramidal orchid)

Furthermore, there are a series of plants which are found in any of these three alliances, but are typical of none of them. These "companion" species, as they are called by botanists, are:

>*Pinus halepensis* (Aleppo pine)
>*Cistus albidus* (grey-leaved cistus)
>*Cistus salvifolius* (sage-leaved cistus)
>*Cistus monspeliensis* (narrow-leaved cistus)
>*Smilax aspera* (sarsaparilla)
>*Asphodelus aestivus*
>*Ampelodesmos mauritanica*

It is important to note that the presence of the pine (like that of the cistuses) signifies nothing at all as regards classification of communities, and thus, for example, the expression "pine forest" has no scientific meaning.

Of these three alliances it is the *Quercion ilicis* —the true oak forest— which occupies the land least affected by drought (thus, it is non-existent in Ibiza, Cabrera and the southern part of Majorca where rainfall is scarce) and by man (thus it has tended to take refuge in the mountains where man has been unable or unwilling to clear the land). It is what scientists refer to as a climax, i.e. the final balance obtained in a geobotanical succession. For this reason they believe that the oak forest must have covered a large part of the Balearic Islands in early times. As Chateaubriand said, "forests precede man and deserts follow him". We have not gone so far here (particularly not in comparison with the Spanish mainland which, during its past history, was so violently shorn of trees), but it cannot be denied that the physiognomy of the islands has changed remarkably since the arrival of man.

One peculiarity of the Balearic oak forest is that the vegetation beneath its canopy of trees is relatively poor, particularly in comparison with the *Quercion ilicis* of Catalonia and the south of France. This is partly due to charcoal makers and partly due to the desire to keep the woods themselves clean and passable. But more than anything else it is due to the pigs which were traditionally allowed to forage there. In their search for acorns and particularly for the underground tubers of the *Cyclamen balearicum* (see p. 49), they constantly uprooted the soil, preventing renewal of the vegetation. Sometimes the result is impressive: a high roof of majestic trees and beneath it an immense empty space, like a cathedral, pierced by shafts of light.

Nowadays, however, this situation seems destined to change radically. The charcoal makers have been replaced by the butane gas company; there is no one to clear the forest (except for purposes of property development) and it is more profitable to raise pigs in artificial conditions. One consequence of this has already become a sad reality: the increase in the danger of forest fires.

In any case, it is difficult to predict what the Balearic oak forests will be like twenty years from now.

In places where it is drier and man has caused more destruction, the *Quercion ilicis* has been replaced by the *Oleo-Ceratonion*. This alliance covers the major part of central and southern Majorca and a large part of Minorca. In still drier, inhospitable lands like those between Palma and Sant Telm, parts of the west coast of Majorca and a considerable part of Ibiza, we find the *Rosmarino-Ericion*. In my opinion this is one of the most dramatic alliances to be found in our islands (second only to that found on the cliffsides). You have only to walk across one of the hills of Santa Ponça (Puig Morisca or Puig Revell) in March or April to see the wealth of species which grow in such apparently poor and miserable countryside, and to appreciate the power of adaptation of the plant world around us.

Before leaving this subject, we must mention the importance in Ibiza of an association of kermes oak and mastic consisting of the following plants:

> *Quercus coccifera* (kermes oak)
> *Pistacia lentiscus* (mastic tree or lentisk)
> *Cneorum tricoccon*
> *Rhamnus lycioides*
> *Juniperus phoenicea* v. *lycia* (Phoenician juniper)
> *Arisarum vulgare* (friar's cowl)
> *Daphne gnidium*

You will find the *Rhamnus* and juniper respectively described in the sections on mountain (p. 84) and dune (p. 120) plants.

1. *Rhamnus ludovici-salvatoris*
2. *Crocus minimus* ss. *cambessedesii*
3. *Globularia cambessedesii*
4. *Scutellaria balearica*
5. *Paeonia cambessedesii*
6. *Viola jaubertiana*
7. *Helleborus lividus*
8. *Sibthorpia africana*
9. *Cephalaria balearica* v. *balearica*
10. *Genista cinerea* ssp. *leptoclada*

FIELDS AND ROADSIDES

Other Members of the Daisy Family

Going on now to field and roadside plants, we find four major families which are dominant: the daisy, umbellifer, mustard and grass families. Let us start with those members of the daisy family, or *Compositae*, in the sub-family of the *Tubuliflorae* (see p. 56), which have tubular-shaped flowers in the central disc and tongue-shaped flowers around the edges. One of the first to cover our fields with its yellow flowers —it begins blooming in October— is the field marigold (*Calendula arvensis*) (**62**). It is the wild and smaller brother of the garden marigold (*Calendula officinalis*). A curious feature of this plant is that the fruit, when ripe, have three different shapes: the one on the outer rim of the

head are shaped like a sickle and have tiny hooks (dispersion by animals), the middle ones are winged and boat-shaped (dispersion by the wind), and the inner ones are thinner and worm-like. When spring comes *Chrysanthemum coronarium* (**63**) or crown daisy becomes more dominant. This is a robust (up to 80 cm tall), beautiful plant which would be better appreciated were it not so abundant, particularly in such mundane spots as vacant lots in the centre of Palma. It has two forms: the normal one with entirely yellow inflorescence, and *discolor* with the lateral tongues

62. *Calendula arvensis*. Field marigold.

partly yellow and partly white. At the end of the summer the composite which dominates the edges of the roadways is *Dittrichia* (or *Inula*) *viscosa*, aromatic inula (**64**). It is easy to recognize because it is practically the only plant of its size (50-100 cm) in bloom from August to October, because it is viscous to the touch and because it has a rather unpleasant resinous odour. Somewhat

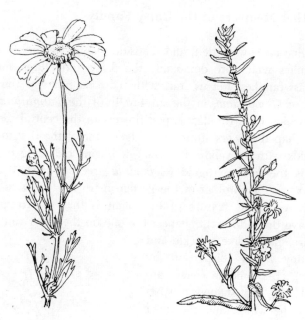

63.   *Chrysanthemum coronarium*. Crown daisy.
64.   *Dittrichia viscosa*. Aromatic inula.

earlier in the summer —in June and July— you can see *Pallenis spinosa* (**65**) in the dry fields. Beneath its yellow, rather flat, head of flowers stretch long, thorny horizontal bracts.

The most important group of *Tubuliflorae*, those with entirely tube-shaped flowers, is that of the thistles. (see p. 58). The most common to our fields is the *Galactites tomentosa* (**66**). The flowers are violet and sometimes white (with longer flowers on the outside) whilst the leaves have a white line down the centre. The star thistle (*Centaurea calcitrapa*) with its narrow pink head

65. *Pallenis spinosa.*   66. *Galactites tomentosa.*

surrounded by very thorny bracts is also fairly common. We also have the *Cynara cardunculus* or cardoon (**67**) with large, violet floral heads and still larger thorny bracts and very large, thorny leaves. This is the wild brother of the cultivated artichoke, *Cynara scolymus.* In Majorca it is sometimes called the "cheese thistle" because its flowers contain an active coagulant which is used to curdle milk in preparing cheese. The women who pick the plant never touch the rare, white-blossomed examples —var. *albiflora*— because they know it does not contain this coagulant.

Despite the fact that the Majorcans call it "pig's snout", perhaps the most beautiful of the *Compositae* of the subfamily *Liguliflorae* is the *Urospermum dalechampii* (**68**). This common name is also used to designate its brother, *Urospermum picroides,* which is very similar in appearance. Both plants have single, very large floral heads of a sulphurous yellow which are recognizable from a distance. They can be told apart because the stem and leaves of the former are covered with soft hairs, the leaves are more deeply cut and the final segment is considerably larger; while the latter is covered with rougher hairs and has leaves that are slightly wavy and bordered with tiny teeth. Another fairly common *Liguliflora* is *Reichardia picroides* which is recognizable by its three types of leaves: the large, irregularly dentated radical leaves (which arise from ground level); the smaller, non-divided (sometimes dentated) cauline leaves (which sprout from the stem) and, highest up, tiny little leaflets that are scarcely more than scales. Perhaps as lovely as "pig's snout" is chicory (*Cichorium*

67. *Cynara cardunculus.* Cardoon.   68. *Urospermum dalechampii.*

intybus) (**69**) which has given the sub-family of *Liguliflorae* its synonym of *Cichoreae*. The floral head —which usually opens only in the morning and on sunny days— is a distinctive sky blue color. In many countries the leaves are used in salads and the root is used as a coffee substitute (or additive). A close relative of this plant is *Cichorium endivia* which gives the escarole and endive of commerce. The sow-thistles, *Sonchus oleraceus, S. tenerrimus* and *S. asper* take their Majorcan name of *lletsó* or "milk plant" from the fact that, like all plants of this subfamily, they contain a milky juice. This is a latex which gives them an astringent taste which is particularly nice in salads.

The Umbellifer, Mustard and Grass Families

Some of the *Umbelliferae* —the flowers of which are grouped in the shape of an umbrella or parasol and which include edible species such as celery, parsley and aniseed, as well as the carrot and fennel described below— grow to amazing proportions. The winner as far as size is concerned is the giant fennel (*Ferula communis*) which, when full grown, is 2-3 metres tall. It has been cited in all the Balearic Islands (in Majorca I have seen it only at Puig Roig, Ternelles and Cap d'es Pinar, although it has been reported everywhere from Esporles to Capdepera), but it is most

69. *Cichorium intybus.* Chicory.   70.   *Foeniculum vulgare.* Common fennel.

abundant in Cabrera. As soon as you enter the harbor there you see it blooming on the crests of the surrounding hills.

Another umbellifer which may grow to a height of more than 2 metres is common fennel (*Foeniculum vulgare*) (**70**), but it is a much more slender and nebulous plant, never having as thick a stem as the giant fennel. Common fennel is very abundant, but even more abundant is the wild carrot or Queen Anne's lace, *Daucus carota* (**71**). Although it is smaller —usually less than 5 feet tall— it is very attractive with its huge umbels that look like big white plates.

71. *Daucus carota*. Wild carrot, Queen Anne's lace.
72. *Smyrnium olusatrum*. Alexanders.

Neither as edible nor, thank God, as common is a rather similar umbellifer which is easily recognizable by the reddish spots on its stem. This is the famous hemlock (*Conium maculatum*), known since antiquity for its poisonous properties (the preparation Socrates drank came from this plant). Alexanders —*Smyrnium olusatrum* (**72**) is an odd-shaped umbellifer with large, trifoliate leaves connected to the stem by a wide, grooved sheath. It blooms early —in the month of March and sometimes even earlier. It is curious that the names in English and in Majorcan (*aleixandri* or often the plural form, *aleixandris*) are the same. It is believed that both names come from the famous Greek conqueror although no one really knows what connection there could be between the historic figure and the plant, nor how it wound up affecting only these two languages. While alexanders seek cool and shady places *Kundmannia sicula* (**73**) seeks dry, sunny spots. It also blooms later —when the hot days begin. It has a yellow flower like fennel, but the plant is smaller (30-70 cm.) and the leaves are not laciniate, but divided into oval, toothed leaflets.

The *cruciferae* or mustard family also includes many species which are important to man. Among them are cabbage, cauliflower, Brussels sprout, black mustard (see p. 90) where we discuss the genus *Brassica* from which these four come), white mustard, radish (which we will discuss in a moment), and the watercress —*Nasturtium officinale*— which is found near streams and irrigation canals throughout the islands. This is almost certainly the family which is easiest for the beginner to recognize. Almost all its members have the same shaped flower with 6 stamens, the outer two of which are always shorter than the others, and 4 petals

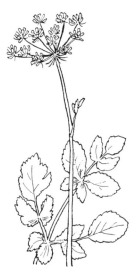

73. *Kundmannia sicula.*

which start out narrow and vertical (the part known as the "claw") and gradually become wider and horizontal, giving the flower the shape of a cross, whence the Latin family name. Perhaps the most common member of the family, both here and in a large part of Europe, is charlock (*Sinapis arvensis*) which sometimes constitutes a real plague in cultivated fields with its masses of bright yellow flowers. It is a brother to the white mustard (*Sinapis alba*) cultivated in other parts of Europe. Also common, but without yet being a pest is wild radish (*Raphanus raphanistrum*) with its dirty white flower veined with lilac, cousin of the cultivated radish (*Raphanus sativus*). Another white flower with lilac-colored veins is the white rocket, *Diplotaxis erucoides*, but this has lobed leaves and straight fruit (only slightly wavy at the margins); while the basal leaves of the former are divided all the way in to the mid-rib (with the final section a good deal larger than the others) and the fruit consists of a series of little beads like a rosary. The commonest crucifer growing by the sides of village roads and streets is the tiny *Capsella bursa-pastoris*, whose English name of "shepherd's-purse" is a translation of the Latin name, and refers to its typical heart-shape fruit.

Sisymbrium officinale, or hedge mustard, is almost as common, but much stranger looking with its yellow flower and its fruit growing flat against the stem. Moreover the central stalk is practically vertical while the other floral stems are completely horizontal. Its designation *officinale* indicates that it was used in apothecaries' "offices" (shops) as a medicinal plant. And indeed, as Palau explains, it was "widely recommended against throat afflictions; singers made great use of it to preserve and clarify the voice".

The *gramineae* or grass family is probably the most important family of all, at least for mankind. It provides the cereals —wheat, millet, corn, barley, oats, rice— and the pasturage which is converted into meat and wool, as well as sugar, bamboo, cane, etc. But it is a rather complicated family from a botanical point of view, with many species, not always easily separable, and a whole special terminology. For this reason and in order to save space, we shall confine ourselves here to the most common species.

Oats is the name for two species which are difficult to tell apart: *Avena sterilis* and *Avena barbata* (**80**), but easy to recognize by their well-separated spikelets, which droop downwards, ending in two long filaments. They are closely related to *Avena sativa* or cultivated oats.

Another species easy to recognize is *Hyparrhenia hirta* (**74**) (=*Andropogon hirtus*), which is quite tall (50-150 cm) with irregular lateral stalks that always end in two final v-shaped spikes, and which blooms almost all year long.

74. *Hyparrhenia hirta.*
75. *Dactylis glomerata.*
76. *Brachypodium retusum.*
77. *Hordeum murinum.* Wall barley.
78. *Poa annua.* Meadow grass.
79. *Piptatherum miliaceum.*
80. *Avena.* Wild oats.
81. *Stipa.*
82. *Cynodon dactylon.* Bermuda grass.

The most typical grass of the Mediterranean oak forest is *Brachypodium retusum* (=*B. ramosum*) (**76**) (20-60 cm) which has a multitude of tiny, narrow leaves that arise almost horizontally from the main stalk. Its relative, *Brachypodium phoenicoides* (30-80 cm), is somewhat less common. Its leaves are larger and point more upwards. Another common grass is *Piptatherum miliaceum* (=*Oryzopsis miliacea*) (**79**) (60-130 cm) with a great number of tiny spikes atop a highly ramified stalk. The *Dactylis glomerata* (**75**) (40-150 cm) has an equally large number of spikelets, but they are stubbier and more moustache-shaped.

Hordeum murinum (**77**), ssp. *leporinum* (10-50 cm), or wall barley, has only a single, rather long and large spike. The Majorcans commonly refer to it as "arrows" because of the shape of its spikelets and their habit of sticking to clothes. It is a close relative of cultivated barley, *Hordeum vulgare*.

Other species with a single spike are *Stipa offneri* (=*S. juncea*) (**81**) (40-80 cm) and *Stipa capensis* (= *S. retorta*) (20-60 cm) which are difficult to tell apart without going into technical details. Their single spikes have very long (5-15 cm) spirally twisted hairs (which are actually the awns of the spikelets). These are both relatives of *Stipa tenacissima*, esparto grass, an Ibero-Mauritanian plant which is found in the Balearic Islands only on the island of Espartar and a few places near the Ibizan coast as well as in Ses Marjades at Artrutx (Minorca) where it was possibly introduced by man.

The smallest (2-30 cm) of the common grasses is *Poa annua* (**78**), annual meadow-grass. Like *Piptatherum miliaceum* it has numerous tiny spikelets on a many-branched stalk, but the entire plant is smaller and more slender. Bermuda-grass, *Cynodon dactylon* (**82**), is almost as small. It is easy to recognize by its 2-6 long slender spikelets (which are often purple-coloured) which all arise from the same point at the tip of the stem.

Other Families

Of the common plants belonging to other families perhaps the best known is the common poppy (*Papaver rhoeas*) which turns entire fields bright red in the month of June. It has two slightly smaller and not so common relatives which are also found in the fields —*Papaver dubium* and *Papaver hybridum.* On waste ground (and cultivated in double-blossomed form in gardens) we find *Papaver somniferum* which until recently was used as a medicinal plant by Majorcan peasants who where quite unaware that it is from this plant that opium and its derivates are extracted. Another plant which covers entire fields, particularly around Palma, is Cape sorrel or Bermuda buttercup, *Oxalis pes-caprae*

(= *O. cernua*) (**83**). It has trifoliate leaves like clover and 5-petalled yellow flowers which bloom as early as February, but only open on sunny days. The stems have a slightly sour taste, but are nonetheless pleasant to chew on. The plant is not a native of Europe. It was brought from the Cape of Good Hope towards the end of the 18th Century and has spread throughout the Mediterranean, sometimes to such an extent that it is a real menace.

In the fields a very common climbing plant is the bindweed, of which there are two common species here: field bindweed, *Convolvulus arvensis* (**84**), with leaves the

83.   *Oxalis pes-caprae.* Cape sorrel, Bermuda buttercup.

shape of an arrowhead, and mallow-leaved bindweed, *Convolvulus altheoides* (**85**) with deeply lobed leaves. The reader must not be influenced by the colour of the flower which varies greatly in both species and cannot be used for purposes of identification. Also in the *Convulvulaceae* family we have two well-known cultivated plants, the sweet potato (*Ipomoea batatas*) and the morning glory (*Ipomoea purpurea*) which covers village walls with its blue and lavender flowers.

Within the sub-family *Asphodeloideae* of the lily family (see pages 40 and 47) there are three notable representatives of the genus *Allium* (the genus of onions and garlic). The biggest and most spectacular is the wild leek, *Allium ampeloprasum,* which grows up to a metre high and has little pink flowers clustered in a full round head that measures 7-10 cm. in diameter.

84.   *Convulvulus arvensis*. Field bindweed.
85.   *Convulvulus altheoides*. Mallow-leaved bindweed.

The rose garlic, *Allium roseum,* which frequently grows along the edges of roads, also has a pink flower, but the entire plant is shorter (15-40 cm.) and the floral heads are flatter. In cooler, shady places we will find *Allium triquetrum* (**86**) which has little white flowers that are more widely spaced and hang downwards; but it is mainly identifiable by its stem, which has a triangular cross section, as indicated by its scientific name. These three plants smell quite strongly of garlic, particularly the green parts.

The oddest shaped genus within this sub-family is *Muscari,* of which two species are common in the Balearic Islands: *Muscari comosum,* tassel hyacinth (**87**), and *Muscari neglectum* (= *M. racemosum*) or grape hyacinth (**88**). The first, and most common, has a spike with three types of flowers: in the middle, the ordinary flowers in the shape of a little closed bell, blackish-purple

86. *Allium triquetrum.*
87. *Muscari comosum.* Tassel hyacinth.
88. *Muscari neglectum.* Grape hyacinth.

in colour, and pointing upwards; below, already wilted flowers, brown in colour and stretched out horizontally; on top, small sterile flowers of a pale violet colour and with fairly long peduncles, forming a sort of umbel. The second has a shorter stalk, with all the flowers alike-blue, slightly inflated, and drooping.

Within the sub-family *Papilionaceae* of the pea family (see pages 33 and 54) there is one representative that can deceive the beginner. If you walk through untilled Majorcan fields in the month of June you will sometimes see an entire carpet of little plants measuring 5-25 cm. in height, each one with a round floral head composed of a series of reddish stars. But these stars, which look like flowers, are the dried and opened calyxes of the flowers which bloomed several weeks earlier and which would have permitted you to identify the plant as *Trifolium stellatum,* starry clover. In the oak forests there are fields which have been long untilled and here we find a pink-blossomed member of the *Papilionaceae,* the shape of which is well described by its name of *Ononis spinosa* or spiny restharrow. In these same fields, and also in the seaside dunes we find a plant of the same genus, but with a yellow flower. It grows into a shrub 40-60 cm. high and can be recognized by its covering of glandular hairs which make it sticky to the touch. This is *Ononis natrix* or large yellow restharrow.

Also sticky to the touch and growing in dry fields is the *Bellardia trixago* which belongs to the family *Scrophulariaceae.* This is a relative of the garden snapdragon, and is somewhat similar, with white flowers whose upper lip is pink and yellow. In the fields and also on the rocky coast you can see one of the most common plants of our islands, *Anagallis arvensis,* scarlet pimpernel. It is a small, trailing plant with a square stem, opposite, pointed leaves and solitary small 5-petalled flowers of a deep blue (or scarlet).

For someone really keen on botany, even waste ground —as for instance that resulting from building or road construction— can be of interest. One of the strangest plants we can find there is *Ecballium elaterium,* squirting cucumber, which belongs to the same family —the *Cucurbitaceae*— as the cultivated cucumber, melons, squash and watermelon. Its name comes from its extraordinary way of dispersing its seed. The ripe fruit (which looks like a small hairy melon) builds up a fairly high degree of internal pressure, and when it falls, from the hole where it detached from its stalk, a mixture of liquid and seed is shot out to a distance of two or more metres. This mini-explosion can be provoked by a stick, but be careful not to get the liquid in your face as it can irritate the eyes.

A genus which is a garden plant in other countries and quite neglected here in the islands is *Reseda,* mignonette, with its long floral spikes, each flower of which, when seen at close range, has laciniate petals. *Reseda alba,* white mignonette, is the most common. There are two species which have yellow flowers: *Reseda lutea,* wild mignonette, with its deeply lobed leaves and *Reseda luteola,* dyer's rocket, or weld, with its simple leaf.

This is by no means a complete description of the plants which grow in the fields, roadsides and waste ground of the Balearics. We have ignored entire families as important as the *Geraniaceae* (geranium), *Plantaginaceae* (plantain) and *Malvaceae* (mallow), but we have two excuses for doing so. One is the desire to keep this book brief and the other is that almost all these plants are pan-European and thus easily identifiable with the aid of the manuals listed in the bibliography. For similar reasons I have not discussed plant communities (in addition to the fact that here the matter of alliances and associations is a good deal more complicated).

11. *Bupleurum barceloi*
12. *Hypericum cambessedesii*
13. *Thymus richardii* ssp. *richardii*
14. *Galium crespianum*
15. *Brassica balearica*

16. *Erodium reichardii*
17. *Senecio rodriguezii*
18. *Genista acanthoclada* v. *balearica*
19. *Naufraga balearica*
20. *Primula vulgaris* ssp. *balearica*

MOUNTAINS AND WALLS

Mountain slopes

When we begin climbing up towards the mountains, particularly in the northwestern mountain range of Majorca, the situation changes radically. Suddenly we begin finding plants (and even entire associations) which are endemic to the Balearic Islands and others of Tyrrhenian or Ibero-Mauritanian distribution, and many of our floras are no longer of any use. The situation of plant communities, on the other hand, becomes clearer: there are fewer of them and they are more clearly defined.

Let us begin with the most common alliance of these mountains, the *Hypericion balearici,* which takes its name from the endemic St. John's-wort, *Hypericum balearicum* (**89**). This shrub has yellow flowers with numerous stamens like other species of

89. *Hypericum balearicum.*   90. *Teucrium asiaticum.*

91. *Pastinaca lucida.*

Hypericum, but the young branches are square-sectioned and covered, like the leaves, with glandular vesicles which make them sticky to the touch and give them their characteristic resinous odour. Also endemic, despite its botanical name, is *Teucrium asiaticum* [9] (**90**). It has the typical flower of the germanders (see p. 55), and narrow leaves which, when bruised, give off a strong medicinal smell both distinctive and unpleasant. Stronger smelling still is another endemic plant, *Pastinaca lucida* (**91**) which the locals have baptized stink weed, devil's cabbage or infernal fig. Nonetheless, the plant is a sister to wild parsnip, *Pastinaca sativa.* Both are biennial umbellifers which sprout leaves the first year and a flowering stem in the second. In our endemic species the lower leaves are large and simple, but as they ascend the stem they become smaller and divided into anything from 3-7 segments. Another aromatic plant typical of this alliance is lavender cotton (*Santolina chamaecyparissus*), but in this case the fragrance is pleasant and much esteemed. Still, it is curious that this composite which is widely distributed throughout central and southern Europe is restricted in Majorca to parts of the northwest mountain range from Es Teix to Puig Tomir. At the same time there is a subspecies, *magonica,* the "chamomile of Mahon" as it is know locally, which is found on the east coast of Minorca, at Capdepera and Santa Ponça in Majorca, and on the tiny island of Es Vedrà near Ibiza,

[9] This plant was formerly known as *T. lancifolium,* which was more descriptive and less absurd, but then it was realized that the name *T. asiaticum* —doubtless due to a confusion on the part of Linnaeus— was older, and therefore, according to the rules of taxonomic nomenclature, should be given precedence. For other cases caused by the same sort of confusion, see pages 85 and 92.

and which is endemic. Another endemic plant is the most attractive of this alliance, the peony, *Paeonia cambessedesii* [10] (photo no. 5). The bright red flower, 6-10 cm. in diameter, would do honors to any garden. The horn-shaped fruit is also attractive, particularly when it is half-opened and you can see the mixture of ripe black seeds and the immature seeds which are almost as brilliant a red as the flower. This peony shares a common trait with other plants which are endemic to the Balearis Islands: the underside of the leaves is purple.[11] The endemic *Scutellaria balearica* (photo no. 4), a small creeping labiate with long-stemmed opposite leaves and tiny purple axillary flowers has this same distinctive characteristic.

Two associations are distinguishable in the *Hypericion balearici*. The first is the *Pastinacetum lucidae*, largely characterized by:

Pastinaca lucida
Teucrium asiaticum
Paeonia cambessedesii
Scutellaria balearica

The other association included in the *Hypericion* is the *Teucrietum subspinosi*, largely typified by two endemic plants in the shape of pin cushions. Both of these plants are well-known to hikers. One is the *Teucrium subspinosum* (92) which gives its name to the association and the other is the *Astragalus balearicus* (= *A. poterium*) (93). When they are in bloom it is easy to see that they belong to different families. The former is a member of the mint family, with the characteristic *Teucrium* flower (see pp. 55 and 82) and the second belongs to the *Papilionaceae* (pp. 33 and 54) with a small, long and narrow flower. But when

---

[10]   Named after the first botanist who made a really serious study of the flora of the Balearic Islands, Jacob Cambessèdes (1799-1863). It is said that he obtained specimens of plants from inaccessible cliffsides by shooting them down with a shotgun.

[11]   Like *Cyclamen balearicum* (p. 49), the *Senecio rodriguezii* (p. 112) and the Tyrrhenian *Micromeria filiformis* (p. 92). This is apparently due to the presence of a flavonoid. The phenomenon occurs in Majorca and Minorca (and even Corsica), but not in Ibiza.

they are not in bloom they are an example of convergent evolution which can confuse the beginner. The *Teucrium* is whiter and its spines are lateral formations of the twigs; the *Astragalus,* on the other hand, is dark green and its spines are the hardened rachis of the leaves. In other words, the lateral leaflets fall from the compound leaf, leaving only the central axis which turns hard and sharp. The evolution towards spiny pin cushions is an adaptation to the wind and is therefore typical throughout the world of mountainous zones (even sarsaparilla —see p. 42— adopts this form in the mountains) and rocky coasts —see p. 110—. However it is a protection not only against the wind, but also against herbivorous animals, and each plant may actually com-

92. *Teucrium subspinosum.*   93. *Astragalus balearicus.*

prise a micro-habitat, offering its own protection to other small plants and insects. A plant which has only completed half this process of evolution —it is spiny but has not yet acquired the compact pin cushion shape, being more of a shrub which has been battered and deformed by the wind— is *Rhamnus lycioides* of Majorca and Ibiza (it is not found in Minorca). It resembles a small olive, thorny and with tiny leaves (although this last trait may vary considerably). In the mountains of Majorca it is to be found mostly on Es Teix and Galatzó. Variety *palaui* of rosemary (see p. 36) is also to be found battered and deformed by the wind.

Of more localized plants the one with the strangest and most discontinuous distribution is the endemic *Thymelaea myrtifolia* (= *T. velutina*) (**94**). It is found in three places: 1) in the northwest mountains from Es Teix to Puig Roig; 2) on the seaside dunes of Ca'n Picafort and Arenal (where its existence is threatened by resort construction), and in one spot near Peguera; 3) in a dozen or so places near the coast of Minorca. It is easy to recognize by its small round and furry leaves (which give a silvery tone to the entire plant), arranged closely along the stem.

94. *Thymelaea myrtifolia.*

Still more restricted is *Helichrysum italicum* (= *H. angustifolium*) ssp. *microphyllum* which is found only on the mountains of Puig Major, Maçanella and Galileu, and on the island of Dragonera. It resembles its coastal brother (p. 112), but with leaves which (as indicated a little too insistently by its scientific names) are very small and narrow.

Of the aforementioned plants, those which are typical of the *Teucrietum subspinosi* are:

> *Teucrium subspinosum*
> *Astragalus balearicus*
> *Rosmarinus officinalis*, var. *palaui* (rosemary)
> *Thymelaea myrtifolia*
> *Helichrysum italicum* ssp. *microphyllum*

Two other attractive endemic plants are often associated with them. The first is the absurdly named *Phlomis italica* (**95**) (see Note no. 9). Without its flower it resembles a grey-leaved cistus with lanceolate leaves, but its flowers are unmistakably of the mint family: pink, curved and grouped in whorls. The other is an endemic foxglove, *Digitalis dubia* (**96**), with a thimble-shaped flower which is usually pink with purple spots but which, in some

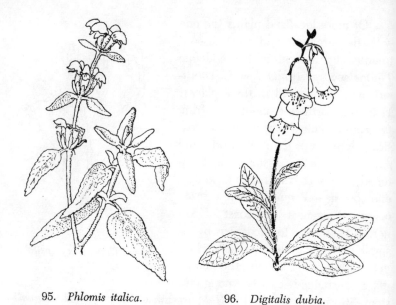

95. *Phlomis italica.*   96. *Digitalis dubia.*

cases, may be entirely white. The common foxglove of west and central Europe, *Digitalis purpurea,* yields the digitalis used in medicine for controlling the heartbeat. Used by laymen it is a poison which can stop the heart. Although the Balearic species has fewer dangerous glycosides, it could still be the islands' most poisonous plant. These two endemic plants are only to be found in the northwest mountains of Majorca, the hills of Artà, and in Minorca (the second also in Cabrera). A curious plant associated with the same alliance is the *Helleborus foetidus* var. *balearicus* (stinking hellebore), an endemic variety of a species which is found from Portugal to Germany. It has palmate leaves and green drooping flowers. It is cited in all botany books as an example of a plant which has maintained its intermediate leaves between the large lower leaves and the floral bracts, which permits an entire evolutionary process to be observed in a single species. Closely related is *Helleborus lividus,* ssp. *lividus* (photo no. 7), an endemic sub-species of a Tyrrhenian species. It can be distinguished from the former by its lower leaves: *foetidus* has leaves which are divided into 7-11 leaflets while in *lividus* they are only divided into 3.

Both plants are to be found in the northwest mountains of Majorca (the latter, which also exists on Cabrera, generally in shadier spots).

Within this alliance of the *Hypericion balearici* we find the greatest abundance of *Ampelodesmos mauritanica* which covers large expanses of our mountains with its greenery. Also associated with this alliance is the carline thistle, *Carlina corymbosa* (see p. 58). Furthermore, in areas of mountain scree we find two little plants which are locally referred to as "wild saffron" and which closely resemble one another in shape and in their autumn blooming, but which in fact belong to different families. One, the endemic *Crocus cambessedesii* (Photo no. 2) belongs to the iris family and is a relative of the *Crocus sativus*, the stigmas of which yield the saffron used in cooking. The other, the *Merendera filifolia* (a species found only in Bouches-du-Rhône in France, the Algarve in Portugal, and Algeria) belongs to the lily family and is the only representative of the sub-family *Colchiceae* (see p. 40). In addition to family differences (the former has 3 stamens and inferior ovary while the latter has 6 stamens and superior ovary) these plants can be told apart by their flowers: the former has a whitish flower with dark lines on the outer rim of the outside petals while the latter is of a solid pinkish-lavender colour. It is also in these rocky grounds that we find the most spectacular representative of the lily family, the sea squill, *Urginea* (or *Scilla*) *maritima*. It has an enormous bulb (up to 13 cm. in diameter) from which a single, long (1 - 1.5 m.) flowering spike appears in September. Once the spike has died, beautiful shiny green leaves begin to appear. These last throughout the winter, but die before the new spike sprouts the following summer.

Cliffs

All the plants we have described in the foregoing section grow where there is a minimum of soil, no matter how poor, and in places where it is normal for vegetation to exist, even though it may seem odd that there should be so much interesting growth. On the other hand, the most amazing habitat, for me at least, of the Balearic mountains, is that of the cliff-faces. Here, on vertical walls of calcareous rock we find a wealth of species (many of which are endemic and a certain number of which are northern plants which have taken refuge here) which range from tiny grasses to small trees two or three metres tall. How they survive and reproduce is almost inconceivable. They all grow in the compost formed from the decomposition of smaller plants (mosses, etc.), compost which accumulates in the fissures of the rocks, and the larger the fissure, the more can accumulate, thus permitting the growth even of small trees. Furthermore, there are plants like the *Brassica balearica* (see following page), the roots of which spread down inside the fissures to such an extent that examples growing one or two metres apart may belong to the same individual plant. Naturally, these plants are well-protected from any type of herbivorous animal, including even the most intrepid mountain goat. But it is difficult to understand how they can withstand the onslaught of the wind, how they can find enough moisture (especially in the summer) and sufficient nourishment, and how enough seed can reach just the right (and so tiny) habitat in order to continue the species. However, it seems that Nature is not even aware of these problems because the cliff faces, particularly in the mountains of Majorca, offer a wealth of plants, many of which are surprisingly beautiful.

One of the most beautiful of all of them is the endemic *Helichrysum ambiguum* (= *H. lamarckii*) (**97**) with its dense rosette of silvery leaves that contrast with its yellow floral heads clustered in a sort of umbel. It is found throughout the northwest Majorcan mountains from Formentor to Dragonera, near Artà, and on Mount Toro in Minorca. Less common, and not as attractive as its relative, is *Helichrysum fontanesii*, which is not as silvery and does not have the rosette of basal leaves. It is an Ibero-Mauritanian species found in the Balearics only in the wildest parts of the northwestern mountain range of Majorca, and on the norther cliffs (in addition to a few other localities) of Ibiza's coast. The most common of the *Compositae* found on the cliffs is the endemic *Crepis triasii* (**98**). It has a yellow, sow-thistle-like lower, and its leaves, toothed at intervals of approximately one every centimetre, grow flat against the rocks. It is found throughout the northwestern mountains of Majorca, near Artà and in the southern half of Minorca.

On the cliffs, as on the plains (see p. 59), there are three species which appear to be *Compositae*, but are not. One of them, *Globularia cambessedesii* (photo no. 3) is a relative of *Globularia alypum* of the plains (see pp. 36 and 59) and is endemic to the mountains of Majorca. The long leaves, slightly turned up

97. *Helichrysum ambiguum.*   98. **Crepis triasii.**

at the margins, are a shiny dark green, and the blue floral heads are large (about 3.5 cm. in diameter). *Scabiosa cretica* (**99**), relative of the *Scabiosa atropurpurea* of the plains (see p. 59) also has a blue floral head, but its leaves are silvery (though not as much so as those of *Helichrysum ambiguum*). From the same family (*Dipsacaceae*) we have *Cephalaria squamiflora* ssp. *balearica* (= *C. balearica*) (Photo no. 9), a Tyrrhenian subspecies (formerly

regarded as a species) of which here we have the endemic var
balearica. Its leaves are large, shiny and dentated and its lovely
white floral heads bloom late, usually in August.

There are two species which are covered in a mass of flower
in the spring and when seen from afar appear as splotches o
yellow on the grey cliffsides. One of them is the wild cabbage

99. *Scabiosa cretica.*   100. *Brassica balearica.*

Brassica balearica (**100**) (Photo no. 15) (see page 71), close relative of the edible cabbage, *Brassica oleracea,* and a species
which is endemic to the Majorcan mountains. It has a somewhat
fleshy leaf, lobed like an oak leaf, and the typical cabbage flower.
The other plant is *Hippocrepis balearica* (**101**): endemic to the
three largest of the Balearic Islands. In Majorca it is commonly
called "cliff violet" which is strange because it bears absolutely
no resemblance to a violet, and in Ibiza it is called "wild lentil"
(a somewhat more realistic name because both this plant and the
lentil are members of the pea family and have similar leaves). The

scientific name is more descriptive still. In Greek, *krepis* means "shoe" and *hippos* means "horse" and the name refers to the legume which has the odd shape of a series of horseshoes. In any case, it is unmistakable — it is the only cliffside plant with yellow flowers and pinnate leaves, i.e. leaves divided into a number (5-10 pairs) of lateral leaflets. The other cliffside member of the pea family is *Genista cinerea* ssp. *leptoclada* (Photo no. 10) which also has a yellow flower, but one that is completely different in appearance. It is a shrub with a multitude of somewhat silvery vertical branches (one scarcely notices the small, entire leaves), which at a distance looks like a joint-pine (see p. 32). The sub-species grows in the northwestern mountains of Majorca and in some parts of the S.E. Spanish province of Murcia, and is thus another quasi-endemic plant.

There are two interesting umbellifers among the smaller, less showy plants. One is *Pimpinella tragium* var. *balearica*, the endemic variety of a species quite widespread throughout the south of Europe. It has a white flower, and more than anything looks like a parsley plant that has strayed into the mountains. Outside the northwestern mountains of Majorca, it has been cited from the Talaia Moreia of Artà and from Mount Randa. When the other umbellifer, *Bupleurum barceloi* (Photo no. 11), is seen without its flowers, the shape and position of the leaves make it seem like a member of the grass family. But its pale yellow inflorescence is unquestionably that of an umbellifer. It is endemic to Majorca's northwest mountain range and Cala d'Albarca in Ibiza. A true grass which grows quite extensively in the northwestern Majorcan mountains is *Sesleria insularis*. This Tyrrhenian species has long leaves and a short spike. A representative of the rose family which also grows on the cliffsides is *Potentilla caulescens* which can be recognized by its palmate leaf, divided into five leaflets and its white five-petalled flower. This species is found from the Alps to the Atlas Mountains, but in the Balearic Islands it grows only in the northwestern mountains of Majorca. The family of the wild madder (see p. 44) has a notable representative in these mountains, as well as near Artà and on the cliffs of Ibiza: this is the endemic *Galium crespianum* (Photo no.

101.   *Hippocrepis balearica.*

14). It has narrow verticillate leaves and the inflorescence is a yellow cloud of tiny flowers.

Five tiny but interesting plants still remain to be described. They are frequently found carpeting the flatter crevices, although the first of them is found almost anywhere in the islands where there is a minimum of soil between two rocks. This is the Tyrrhenian *Micromeria filiformis* with a creeping stalk, opposite leaves about 4 mm. long which are often (but not always) purple on the underside, and with tiny white flowers. Among these carpeting plants there are two sandworts: *Arenaria grandiflora* var. *glabrescens* (endemic variety of a southern European species) and *Arenaria balearica* (which, despite its name, is Tyrrhenian). The first has a small stem and leaves lengthened into a point,[12] while the second appears to have no stem (although it really does have one) and thus seems to be even more of a carpeting plant, and has exceedingly small, ovate leaves (2-4 mm.). They both have small white flowers with five petals and five sepals which might cause them to be confused with the endemic *Erodium reichardii* (Photo no. 16) which also has five petals and five sepals and sometimes has white flowers. But usually each petal of *Erodium* has a violet-colored center vein. Furthermore, its leaves are lobed and larger (5-15 mm.). The leaves of the last plant in this series, the erroneously named (see p. 82) endemic *Sibthorpia africana* (Photo no. 8) also has lobed leaves, but they are much hairier, with hairs at least 1 mm. long, and its flower is bright yellow.

---

[12]   At Maçanella and Puig Major another variety has been found, var. *bolosii*, which is smaller and denser with a shorter, hairy leaf.

In the shadier, more humid parts of the mountains, in places where the soil is deep and the snow stays on the ground a longer time, we will find the beautiful white primrose (*Primula vulgaris,* ssp. *balearica*) (Photo no. 20). This endemic plant is easy to identify with its slightly hairy, large, pale green spatulate leaves. The flower is very fragrant.

Now that we know the individual cliffside plants it would be a good idea to classify them according to their natural communities in order to help clarify our ideas. Our task is made easier by the fact that there are only three associations and it is quite easy to tell them apart.

The first is the *Hippocrepidetum balearicae,* principally characterized by the following species:

Hippocrepis balearica	*Scabiosa cretica*
Genista cinerea ssp. *leptoclada*	*Globularia cambessedesii*
	Bupleurum barceloi

This association is to be found on cliffs almost anywhere from sea level to 900 metres. Higher than that (but being fairly flexible about this figure) on the northern cliff faces, i.e. in colder, higher, windier and shadier parts of the mountains, we find a related association, the *Potentillo-Pimpinelletum balearicum,* the most typical species of which are:

Potentilla caulescens	*Arenaria grandiflora* var. *glabrescens*
Cephalaria squamiflora ssp. *balearica*	*Pimpinella tragium* var. *balearica*

These two associations form part of the alliance *Brassico-Helichrysion rupestris,* of which the following species are typical and may therefore be found in either of the two aforementioned associations:

Crepis triasii	*Brassica balearica*
Helichrysum ambiguum	*Sesleria insularis*
Helichrysum fontanesii	*Digitalis dubia*

The third association is that of the carpeting plants (with the addition of an endemic *Carex* which is small and fairly difficult to identify). This is the *Sibthorpieto-Arenarietum* association, with the following typical plants:

Sibthorphia africana   Erodium reichardii
Arenaria balearica   Carex rorulenta

To conclude, there are two species which may be found in any of the three aforementioned associations:

Micromeria filiformis   Galium crespianum

Stone Walls in Country and Village

Ecologically speaking, cliff faces are related to stone walls of all types, not only the stone walls found in the countryside but even those of any village or city. The *Asplenion glandulosi* alliance is the lowland equivalent of the mountains' *Brassico-Helichrysion rupestris* and both alliances are included in the order of *Asplenietalia glandulosi*. This means that many of the plants we shall now describe will be found on the cliffsides as well as on village walls.

The *Asplenion glandulosi* is characterized primarily by the presence of plants belonging to the class *filicopsida*, which includes ferns and bracken. It might even be said that apart from the bracken (see p. 60 where you will also find a brief description of the class), it is in this habitat where we find almost all the Balearic ferns. Of the eight most common, five have leaves which are divided into separate segments and can be told apart by the shape of these segments. They are:

Asplenium glandulosum (= A. petrarchae) (**105**)
Asplenium onopteris (= A. adiantum-nigrum
     ssp. onopteris) (black spleenwort) (**107**)
Asplenium ruta-muraria (wall rue) (**104**)
Asplenium trichomanes (maidenhair spleenwort) (**103**)
Adiantum capillus-veneris (maidenhair fern) (**106**)

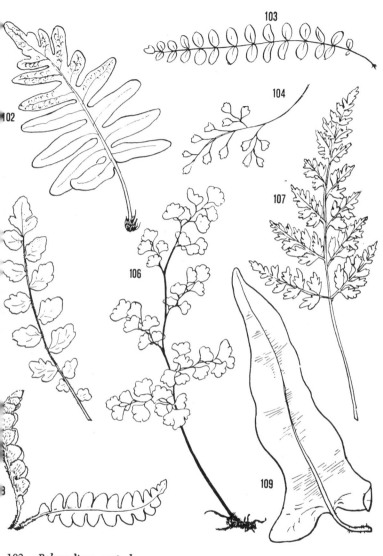

102. *Polypodium australe.*
103. *Asplenium trichomanes.* Maidenhair spleenwort.
104. „ *ruta-muraria.* Wall rue.
105. „ *glandulosum.*
106. *Adiantum capillus-veneris.* Maidenhair fern.
107. *Asplenium onopteris.* Black spleenwort.
108. *Ceterach officinarum.* Rusty-back.
109. *Phyllitis sagittata.*

The other three have lobed, undulate or simple leaves:

> *Polypodium australe* (**102**)
> *Ceterach officinarum* (=*Asplenium ceterach*)
>   (rusty-back) (**108**)
> *Phyllitis sagittata* (= *Scolopendrium hemionitis*) (**109**)

They are not all equally common nor always to be found in the same habitats. Of the *Aspleniums,* for example, the last-named is very common and the first quite rare. The maidenhair fern which we have placed here for convenience, in fact does not belong to the *Asplenion glandulosi,* but is rather found in damp places (wells, springs, humid walls, etc.). Nor does this list include all the ferns of these islands. We could, for example, add the endemic *Asplenium majoricum* from the Sóller region, whose entire rachis —the central axis of the leaf— is shiny brown except for its upper third. There is also the extremely rare hart's-tongue *Phyllitis scolopendrium* (=*Scolopendrium vulgare or officinale*) with leaves up to 60 cm. long, but without the ears of the other *Phyllitis,* which is found in shady places in the high mountains, in S'Entreforc, etc.

The other family well represented in this alliance is the *Crassulaceae* or stonecrop family, with its more or less succulent leaves. The genus *Umbilicus* has less succulent leaves —in fact, they might better be described as "fleshy"— with a distinctive kidney shape and a stem connected to the centre of the leaf rather than to the margin. The most common species is *Umbilicus horizontalis* or pennywort, which is to be found on almost any village wall.

The leaves of the genus *Sedum* are more succulent, so much so that it is often taken for a kind of cactus. Of the four common species, the only one with a yellow flower is *Sedum sediforme* (see p. 12). It is also the most common species and is to be found on rocky hillsides, on walls and even on the roofs of many old houses. The other three species have a pink flower. One of them, *Sedum dasyphyllum* or thick-leaved stonecrop, resembles the previous species in that it is a perennial and also has flowerless sterile stalks at the time of blooming. Of the two emaining species —both of which are annuals— one, *Sedum rubens*, red stonecrop, has cylindrical leaves 1-2 cm. long and the other, *Sedum stellatum*, starry stonecrop, has flatter, slightly toothed leaves. This latter species is the least common of the four, and is to be found only in Majorca's northwest mountain range.

There are three representatives of the daisy family in these habitats. They all belong to the genus *Phagnalon* with tubular yellow flowers (which give the impression of never completely opening) and narrow leaves with white undersides. *Phagnalon sordidum* has small heads (6-7 mm.) clustered in groups of 2-6 and the upperside of the leaves is also white. The other two, *Phagnalon saxatile* and *Phagnalon rupestre* have larger (8-12 mm.) solitary heads and leaves which are green on the upper side. The former is distinguished by having the lower bracts of the head turned outward, as well as by having tiny bracts atop the peduncle just below the head. The latter has no bracts on the peduncle and the bracts of the inflorescence itself are pressed against the head.

A small but very decorative plant is the fumitory (of the poppy family) with its oddly-shaped flowers elongated into a rear pouch or spur, of a white or pink colour with a purplish-black spot. The two commonest species on the Balearic Islands are *Fumaria capreolata*, ramping fumitory, and *Fumaria officinalis*, common fumitory. The first, which has a flower 10-14 mm. long, with lateral sepals of an equal width is found everywhere (cliffs, walls, roads and fields). The latter, with its 7-9 mm. flower and much narrower sepals is largely found in cultivated fields and disturbed ground.

Our most decorative (and most useful) wall plant is assuredly the caper (*Capparis spinosa*) with its large attractive flowers (4-6 cm. across). It grows more or less anywhere, on any wall or in any rocky ground, but it flourishes best on old walls (I have seen it in abundance on walls in Palma, Ciutadella and Ibiza). It is also cultivated —particularly in Campos— for the capers themselves, which are the buds (not the berries), collected before opening, and pickled.

7

With the exception of these last three plants, many of th
plants described above will be found on cliffsides, mingling, a
we said before, with others which belong more exclusively to tha
habitat.

Cliffside trees and shrubs

Also to be found —even more amazingly— on the cliffside
is a series of trees and shrubs, which we will list briefly here.

Acer granatense, an Ibero-Mauritanian maple, is the only tre
(other than the fig, see below) of our mountains with lobe
leaves: they have five palmate lobes.

Sorbus aria or whitebeam. A species which grows on th
plains in northern countries, but here it has taken refuge high ir
the mountains. It has large leaves with silvery undersides anc
serrated edges.

Lonicera pyrenaica ssp. *majoricensis.* And endemic subspecie:
of an Ibero-Mauritanian species of honeysuckle. Apart from the
flower and fruit, it bears no resemblance to the ordinary honeysuckle, *Lonicera implexa,* of the oak forest (see p. 44). This
is a shrub (not a vine) with smaller, oval leaves. It is found mainly
on Puig Major and Maçanella, at altitudes of over 1200 metres.

Amelanchier ovalis, snowy mespilus, is a southern European
species. It is a shrub with leaves like the aforementioned *Lonicera*
(3-5 cm.) but serrated. Mainly on Puig Major and Maçanella, and
quite rare.

It is worth noting that these four species are deciduous (this
is rare in the Balearic Islands: there is only one other deciduous
association, see p. 105) and might possibly be the vestige of more
extensive forests of deciduous trees from earlier times.

Another deciduous tree which is sometimes found in the crevices of cliffs, the fig (*Ficus carica*), might be a fugitive from fig
plantations on the plain. Other trees and shrubs —evergreens all
of them— are:

Ilex aquifolium f. *balearica.* Endemic form of the holly which grows extensively in southern and eastern Europe. Its leaves are like those of the oak (this is why the oak is called *Quercus ilex*), but larger and shiny. On the same tree one can find leaves that are both spiny and smooth. It lives quite far inside the deepest vertical crevices in the high mountains.

Taxus baccata, yew. A species which is distributed throughout almost all of Europe, in Asia as far as the Himalayas and in North Africa, but it has become scarce everywhere, as its wood is highly prized and it is a slow-growing tree. In Majorca there are only a few examples at Planícia, Es Teix, Maçanella, Puig Major and Tomir. While they may not be in the crevices themselves, they are always close to them.[13] The sweet-tasting red fruit which is carried away by the birds is the only part of the tree which does not contain the poisonous alkaloid, taxine. According to Polunin, an animal which eats the leaves of this tree will die within a matter of minutes.

Buxus balearica. This is a species of box known with certainty to exist outside Majorca in only a couple of places in the south of Spain and in North Africa. In Majorca it is found throughout the northwest mountain range, not on the cliffs, but on the higher mountain screes. It is also found in the Torrent de Pareis, almost at sea level, and also on Cabrera. Marès and Vigineix maintain that in 1850 there were entire boxwood forests on Es Teix and Maçanella, with trees whose trunks were sometimes as big around as the body of a man. Only two years later they had all been destroyed by woodcutters and charcoal makers. It also seems that many years ago in Pollença and Cabrera there was a cottage industry which produced forks and spoons made of boxwood, a high quality wood also used for wood-engraving. The remaining specimens of box can be recognized by their entire, oval leaves, 3-4 cm. long, often scorched to a sickly green color by the wind.[14]

---

[13] For the reader who has no desire to climb to such inaccessible places, there is a magnificent example in the gardens of Sa Granja and other smaller ones in the gardens of Lluc.

[14] With the exception of specimens located in the Torrent de Pareis which, because they are sheltered, are a beautiful dark green.

Now we come to two species which are usually found on the cliffs, but at lower altitudes (and which are also cultivated in gardens):

Laurus nobilis, laurel or bay tree. A Mediterranean species which grows near damp, shady cliffs. It abounds, for example, in the Torrent de Pareis. It is easy to recognize by its fairly large (8-10 x 2-3 cm.), entire, coriaceous leaves. Nowadays it is well known as a potherb; in classical times it was even better known as a tree sacred to Apollo. And since Apollo was the god of poets, it was used to make literary crowns. Such as the respect in which it was held that Empedocles of Agrigento called it "the supreme tree."

Viburnum tinus, laurustinus. Like the laurel it seeks cool places (there are many examples around the Gorg Blau). It is a dense compact shrub with little white flowers clustered in flat heads.

Endemic plants

In these same cool places we will find two interesting endemic plants. One is *Viola jaubertiana* (Photo no. 6), a little plant that grows on the lateral walls of the shadiest —usually north-facing— ravines (Gorg Blau, S'Entreforc, etc.) with its violet flower and shiny heart-shaped leaves. The other is the *Hypericum cambessedesii* (Photo no. 12) which is found in the beds of mountain streams (S'Entreforc, Coma Freda of Maçanella, etc.) where there is moisture in the subsoil throughout the year. Its flower is identical to that of the other endemic St. John's wort (see p. 81), but the leaves are completely different: longer, flat and a beautiful pale, almost luminescent, green.

Furthermore, in Majorca's northwest mountain range we find ten much rarer endemic plants which are very interesting for the botanist. Below is a list, along with references to the books (see the Bibliography) where the reader can find them illustrated.

First are four mountain plants:

Ranunculus weyleri. This has been cited in only two places: Puig Major and the Atalaia Moreia of Artà, making for a very peculiar discontinuous distribution. Drawing in Marès and Vigineix.

Ligusticum lucidum ssp. *huteri.* Found on the north face of Puig Major. Also cited from the Gorg Blau and Pla de Cúber. It resembles a hemlock that has wandered off into the mountains. Drawing in Colom, *Medio y vida,* p. 91.

Euphorbia fontqueriana. Apart from two rather mysterious citations by Barceló, this tiny spurge is known definitely to grow only in one place in Maçanella. Drawing in Colom, *Biogeografía,* p. 275.

Euphorbia maresii. An equally tiny spurge, of which there are three varieties:

> var. *maresii* in the mountains of Artà and on the peninsulas of Alcúdia and Formentor.
> var. *balearica* on Puig Major and Maçanella (in the same place as the preceding species).
> (At Cap Blanc and Cap Regana a form intermediate between var. *maresii* and var. *balearica* has recently been found.)
> var. *minoricensis* in Minorca, from Cala Morell to Cape Favàritx, and in the Barranc d'Algendar.

Aristolochia bianorii [15] which is found here and there from Sóller to the Formentor lighthouse, as well as Punta Nati in Minorca. Drawing in Colom, *Biogeografía,* p. 267.

Urtica atrovirens, ssp. *bianorii,* a nettle originally known only from one place in the Serra d'Alfàbia but later found at Cosconar, Coll Ciuró, etc. Drawing in Colom, *Biogeografía,* p. 245.

---

[15] Named for its discoverer, Brother Bianor (1859-1920) who left two important collections of plants, now preserved at the La Salle schools in Pont d'Inca and Son Rapinya.

Genista acanthoclada ssp. *balearica* (Photo no. 18), endemic variety of an eastern Mediterranean species (Greece and Crete). Originally known only in the Coll des Coloms pass between Maçanella and Tossals, but then discovered at Mal Pas in Alcúdia, l'Ofre, Sant Telm, etc. It is thorny like its relative, *Genista lucida*, but lower and trailing, and with thicker spines and branches.

Thymus richardii ssp. *richardii* [16] (Photo no. 13), one of the rarer Majorcan endemisms; found only infrequently around Puig Major, Ariant, and the Formentor peninsula.

Pimpinella bicknelli is one of our most noteworthy endemic plants. For many years it was believed to belong to a special genus (called *Spiroceratium*, or *Adarianta* after the place where it was discovered), but nowadays this umbellifer has been returned to the same genus to which it was attributed by its discoverers at the end of the last century (see p. 91 for another *Pimpinella*; anis, *Pimpinella anisum*, is yet another example). For years it was believed to be restricted to Ariant, but since 1950 other localities have gradually been discovered, and it is now known to grow from Ariant to the Torrent de Pareis. Drawing in Colom, *Biogeografía*, p. 281.

Naufraga balearica (Photo no. 19). In 1962, near Cala Sant Vicenç, a Belgian botanist, Professor Duvigneaud, collected a small plant he was unable to identify. Consultations with other experts resulted in the fact that it was not only a species, but also a genus (also belonging to the *Umbelliferae*) completely unknown to science, a surprising occurrence in the latter part of the 20th century in Europe. Then in 1981 it was discovered in Corsica! The plant, however, is so small, grows in such inaccessible places and in such small quantity (in Majorca it has only been found in one 1000-square-yard area of the sea cliffs), that it might eventually be found elsewhere in the Tyrrhenian area.

In this same year of 1981, another endemic umbillifer very similar in appearance to *Naufraga* was found on the northwest coast of Minorca: this was *Apium bermejoi* discovered by the

---

[16]　There is also the ssp. *ebusitanus*, endemic to Ibiza.

young Minorcan botanist, Andreu Bermejo, and classified and described by Lleonard Llorens.

In matters of endemics, Ibiza has three noteworthy species:

Genista dorycnifolia is a non-thorny relative of the *Genista* species described above. It was discovered in 1919 by the great Catalan botanist Font i Quer.

Carduncellus dianius is a handsome non-spiny thistle found on the north coast of Ibiza as well as a few localities in the nearby Denia region of the Spanish mainland.

Silene hifacensis was formerly found on the coastal cliffs of Valencia (Penyal d'Ifac and Cap de Sant Antoni) and of Ibiza (Cala d'Albarca, Illa de S'Espartar, and several other localities). It had disappeared from its mainland sites, but a recent reintroduction by botanists on the Penyal d'Ifac makes it, like the preceding *Carduncellus dianius*, a quasi Ibizan endemic. For drawings, photographs and distribution maps of these three species see the *Nova aportació al coneixement de les plantes d'Eivissa i Formentera* mentioned in the bibliography (Section 15.b).

In Minorca, apart from the endemics mentioned on pp. 110-113, there are two noteworthy species, one extinct in the wild state and the other recently rediscovered.

The former, *Lysimachia minoricensis,* disappeared from its sole locality, the Barranc de Son Boter, many years ago. In the 1950's and again in the 1970's attempts were made to reintroduce it from seeds conserved in various Spanish and central European botanical gardens, but without success. Fortunately, however, the plant is surviving healthily in various private gardens on the islands.

The other species, *Vicia bifoliolata,* for years was thought extinct, until recently it was rediscovered in several localities in northeastern Minorca, which is very good news indeed. The reader can find a drawing of the former in Marès and Vigineix, and a photo of the latter in Vol. IV of Knoche.

BANKS OF STREAMS

Having mentioned deciduous trees, it might be a good idea to describe the only other Balearic alliance —*Populion albae*— where they are to be found. This alliance is extremely rare in the islands: it only exists on the banks of a few streams. The stream just at the entrance to Puigpunyent is a good example. There we find:

Populus nigra (**115**) — black poplar. Fairly large serrated leaves. In other places we find the *Populus alba* (**114**) — white poplar, — with slightly lobed leaves.

Platanus orientalis (**110**) — London plane. Still larger lobed leaves. Bark which peels off in large patches.

Ulmus minor (**113**) — smooth-leaved elm. Not such a large leaf, serrated with an asymmetric base.

Fraxinus angustifolia (**116**) — ash. Pinnate leaves with 5-13 long slender leaflets.

These are the four main trees of the alliance (in Puigpunyent a couple of Lusitanian oaks (**111**) —see p. 16— have somehow managed to work their way in there as well) and it is worth noting that the two firstnamed were introduced by man and it is not even completely certain that the latter two are native to this habitat. Two members of the rose family are also found here. They are:

Crataegus monogyna (**112**), ssp. *brevispina* — hawthorn. A small thorny tree with small, deeply lobed leaves. The flower appears after the leaf. The fruit is a small cherry-like berry.

Prunus spinosa — blackthorn. Twisted shrub with black branches, many of which end in sharp thorns. Small, finely serrated leaves. The flower appears before the leaf does. The blue-black berry is the sloe, from which sloe gin is made.

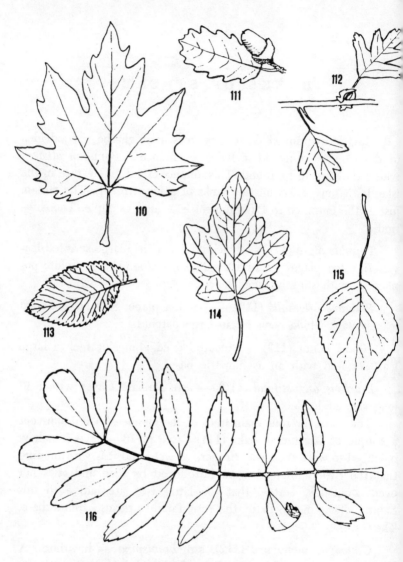

110. *Platanus orientalis*. London plane.
111. *Quercus faginea*. Lusitanian oak.
112. *Crataegus monogyna*. Hawthorn.
113. *Ulmus minor*. Smooth-leaved elm.
114. *Populus alba*. White poplar.
115.   ”   *nigra*. Black poplar.
116. *Fraxinus angustifolia*. Ash.

Both of them are also found outside this alliance, the first by streams or in the mountains and the second in thickets and on walls. It should also be pointed out that the genus *Crataegus* includes the Mediterranean medlar and that *Prunus* contains many of our fruit trees like peach, almond, apricot, cherry and plum.

Under the trees of this alliance we often find a carpet of periwinkles (*Vinca difformis*) with their opposite leaves and their flowers like pale blue miniature windmills. There we also find *Potentilla reptans* or creeping cinquefoil, a relative of the *Potentilla* of the high mountains (see p. 91), identical in shape but with yellow flowers. *Ranunculus ficaria,* ssp. *ficariiformis* or lesser celandine, with heart-shaped leaves and pale yellow flowers, and *Osyris alba* (see p. 32), which grows everywhere.

In many river beds near the sea (Torrent de Pareis, Cala dels Alocs in Minorca, etc.) we find an association characterized by a beautiful shrub, the *Vitex agnus-castus* or chaste tree. It can grow to a height of three meters, has palmate deciduous leaves with long narrow leaflets, and violet-colored flowers in long spikes. In other countries it is often used as a garden plant. From time immemorial this shrub has been associated with chastity. Even in the days of Dioscorides the seeds were said to have the power to calm the "inclinations natural."

Underneath these bushes grows a lovely cousin of the narcissus — especially at the Torrent de Pareis in February or March. This is the summer snowflake, *Leucojum aestivum,* ssp. *pulchellum* which the reader will find illustrated in Colom's two books: *Medio y Vida,* p. 150 and *Biogeografía,* p. 263. Our sub-species is found only in the south of France, Corsica and Sardinia.

In Ibiza alongside the chaste tree, we find the oleander, *Nerium oleander,* so familiar on the other islands as a garden shrub. It is curious to note that Ibiza is the only place in the Balearic Islands where it is to be found in its wild state, and there it grows relatively abundantly.

THE COASTAL REGION

The Rocky Coasts

Now we must move into an entirely different environment: the Balearic coast which, after the mountains, is the zone of greatest botanical interest. Within this zone the rocky coasts have the most to offer the scientist and present the most problems for the beginner. In contrast to the mountain where the plants are fairly well differentiated and easy to identify, on the coasts there are a series of plants with minimal differences which are liable to pose a real puzzle to the amateur botanist. Let us first consider the different parts of the coast.

On the rocky coasts the alliance nearest the sea is the *Crithmo-Limonion* which takes its name from its two most characteristic genera, *Crithmum* and *Limonium*.[17] There only exists a single species of the former in the entire world — *Crithmum maritimum* (**117**), the well-known rock samphire which in Majorca is eaten pickled. It is a low-growing umbellifer with a fleshy leaf that is very easy to recognize. But the genus *Limonium* is just the opposite. There are more than twenty species in the Balearic Islands alone (almost half of which are endemic), not counting a dozen or so hybrids. They all look quite a lot alike, with a basal rosette of spatulate leaves; narrow, jointed branches and tiny flowers, often growing in a line at the end of the upper branches. Apart from this similarity which makes identification difficult, there is also a certain amount of variation within species which is disconcerting to the amateur. My advice is not to get involved

---

17 Which was formerly known as *Statice* and thus the alliance was the *Crithmo-staticion*.

or, if you must, go well-armed with the two studies by Pignatti [18] and the one Leonard Llorens is currently preparing.

The *Crithmo-Limonion* is divided into two associations. Closest to the sea we have the *Limonietum caprariense* which is characterized by the presence of rock-samphire and three species of *Limonium* (mainly the endemic *Limonium caprariense*). They are the only species capable not only of withstanding the force of the wind, but also of resisting the high concentration of salt which rises from the sea. A little further inland, and thus with a slightly lesser concentration of salt, we find the *Launaeetum cervicorni* which gives this zone its real botanical interest.

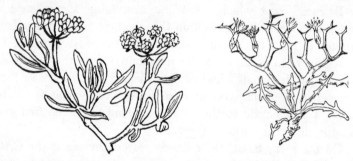

117. *Crithmum maritimum*. Rock samphire.   118. *Launaea cervicornis*.

In a strange parallel with the high mountains, we again find plants in the shape of thorny pin cushions and for the same reason: protection against the battering of the wind. And where the wind blows the hardest (for example, the north coast of Minorca) we find the association most highly developed, and where the wind is not as strong (as, for example, in Ibiza), it is poorer. It takes its name from *Launaea cervicornis* (**118**), an endemic spiny pin cushion of the *Compositae* family which is most common on our coasts, at least in Minorca and Majorca (it does not exist on the other islands). It is unmistakable with its jointed branches

---

[18] One of these is *Studi sulla flora dell'isola de Mallorca* (Baleari), Forli, 1955, and the other is the article "Limonium" in Vol. III of *Flora Europea* (see Bibliography).

in the form of little deer horns (from which it gets its Latin name) and its little sow-thistle-like flowers.[19]

The other member of the *Compositae* among these four endemic "pin cushions" is the *Centaurea balearica*. It is also the rarest of the four: it is cited only in a few places near the three Minorcan capes: Favàritx, Fornells and Cavalleria, and only with any degree of abundance in a spot near the first of these. Many years ago it was spotted on Majorca's Alcudian peninsula, but has never been found there since. It differs from other members of the genus in that its leaves undergo a transformation into thorns; the bracts surrounding the flower heads are also spiny and the flower is purple.

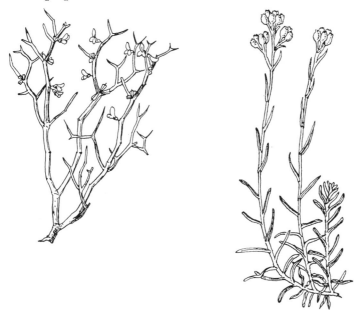

119.   *Anthyllis fulgurans.*   120.   *Helichrysum stoechas.* Everlasting.

The other two endemic "pin cushions" are in the pea family, and both belong to the genus *Anthyllis. Anthyllis fulgurans* (**119**)

---

19   From a taxonomic viewpoint it is so closely related to the *Sonchus* that it was formerly classified within the same genus with the name *Sonchus spinosus* v. *cervicornis.*

is the more widespread of the two. Not only does it grow along the northern coast of Minorca, but is also found at the Formentor lighthouse, at one place near Santa Ponça, and in Cabrera, while the *Anthyllis hermanniae* var. *hystrix* is found only on the island of Minorca (but not solely on the northern coast). The former is larger (it sometimes grows into an almost complete ball, measuring more than three feet in diameter). The branches are brown and grow in a zig-zag pattern, and the flower is pink (or white) and very small (3-4 mm.). The latter tends to be shorter and more compact, with greyish stalks and yellow flowers that measure 5-7 mm.

Within the *Launaeetum* there are also two *Compositae* which are not spiny. *Helichrysum stoechas* (**120**), everlasting, is found more in Majorca than in Minorca. It has tiny whitish leaves with pale yellow dense flower clusters and gives off a distinctive curry smell. Almost only in Minorca we find ssp. *magonica* of *Santolina chamaecyparissus,* lavender cotton (see p. 82).

Within the *Crithmo-Limonion* alliance, and consequently within either of its two associations, there is a series of plants (in addition to several species of *Limonium*) which we will do no more than list briefly:

Senecio rodriguezii (Photo no. 17). A composite endemic to Minorca, the northwest coast of Majorca and the Cap d'es Freu near Artà. It is a small plant (usually no more than 10 cm. tall, although in sometimes grows as high as 30 cm.) with flowers which are pinkish white around the edges and dark pink in the interior, and with leaves which are purple on the underside (see p. 83).

Reichardia picroides. A composite common in the interior of the island (see p. 68).

Asteriscus maritimus with a flower similar to that of the chrysanthemum (see p. 65), but with a simple narrow leaf. The plant itself is denser and often (due to the action of the wind) pressed against the ground.

Desmazeria marina (= *Catapodium loliaceum* or *C. marinum*), sea fern-grass, a low-growing grass (about 10 cm. high) which forms clumps and has long, thin spikes.

The subspecies *hispanicus* of *Daucus carota* (p. 70), from which it differs by being shorter, with a shiner, fleshier leaf, and having convex (rather than flat) floral umbels when in bloom, and flat (rather than concave) umbels when in fruit.

Frankenia hirsuta. A curious plant which resembles a small, almost horizontal heather bush with a white or purple tubular flower. *Frankenia laevis* and *Frankenia pulverulenta* are also to be found, but the three of them are rather difficult to tell apart.

In Minorca, and especially on the Illa d'en Colom, there is a very interesting association which grows in the shelter of this alliance. It is the *Aro-Phillyreetum,* a local version of the *Oleo-Ceratonion* (see p. 61) characterized largely by four plants:

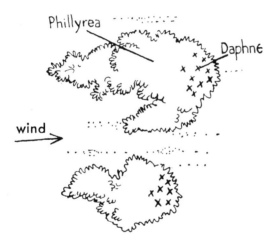

121.   Situation of *Daphne rodriguezii,* according to Oriol de Bolòs.

Phillyrea media var. *rodriguezii.* An endemic Minorcan variety of the phillyrea (see p. 27) with very hard, almost thorny, twigs.

Arum pictum and *Dracunculus muscivorus* (see p. 48).

Daphne rodriguezii (= *D. vellaeoides*). According to Knoche, this plant, together with *Pimpinella bicknelli* and *Hypericum balearicum* is one of the most notable endemic plants of the Balearics, with no near relations or, to put it more exactly, isolated from an evolutionary viewpoint since remote times. Apart from the Illa d'en Colom, it has been found in six other places on the eastern end of Minorca, in at least four of which it has become endangered by property development and by fire. It is a smaller relative of *Daphne gnidium* (see p. 30), growing less than three feet tall and with fragrant purplish flowers slightly tinged with yellow. It practically always grows in the shelter of (or, more precisely, *inside*) the aforementioned *Phillyrea*, as can be seen from the illustration. (**121**).

Beaches and Dunes

Plants growing on beaches and dunes not only have the same problems of wind and excess salt, but also have a soil —the sand— which is not very propitious for preserving moisture and facilitating germination. There are plants whose roots reach exceptionally deep in their search for moisture (like the sea daffodil: see below). There are other plants (particularly grasses) which have selected the rhizome system of reproduction. A rhizome is a stem which grows horizontally just beneath the earth's surface, sprouting new plants at more or less regular intervals. Its placement leads one to confuse it with a root, but its structure and function are clearly those of a stem. In places where the wind has carried away some of the sand from the dunes you can see a network of rhizomes (mingled with the roots of shrubs) which criss-cross in all directions and play an important role in stabilizing the dunes.

Of the three dune grasses which have chosen this system, the best known and the easiest to identify is marram grass, *Ammophila arenaria* ssp. *arundinacea*, (**122**) which is found on all the southern European coasts. It is the tallest of the three (60-100 cm.) with inrolled, prickly leaves and a long (10-25 cm.) cylindrical spike. Sand couch, *Elymus farctus* ssp. *farctus* (= *Agropyron junceum* ssp. *mediterraneum*) is shorter (30-70 cm). Its spike is almost as long (4-20 cm.), but it is not cylindrical;

instead, it consists of a series of tiny spikelets alternating on each side of the central axis. *Sporobolus pungens* (= S. *arenarius*) is much smaller (10-30 cm). It resembles a miniature bamboo, its stem covered with leaves right up to the spike itself, which is very short (2-4 cm). The other member of the grass family to be found here is not typical of the dunes (it can be found in any

grassy place in the islands), but flourishes and grows here quite frequently This is the *Lagurus ovatus* (**123**) or hare's-tail. It is short (10-50 cm.) and is immediately recognizable by its exceptionally hairy, ovoid spike.

The dune plant best known to beachgoers —its prickles make it painful to walk barefoot in the sand— is the sea holly, *Eryngium maritimum* (**124**), brother of the field eryngo (see p. 59). As we mentioned then, it is not a thistle, but an umbe- llifer, with an inflorescence

122. *Ammophila arenaria.* Marram grass.
123. *Lagurus ovatus.* Hare's tail.

which, when in full bloom, is pale blue, as are the surrounding bracts. Insects are attracted by this and seem to find the plant quite to their liking. Humans prefer the sea daffodil, *Pancratium maritimum* (**125**), with its beautiful fragrant white flower, so surprising among such aridity. It is also interesting to note that the fruit (which appears very quickly after the flowering) is equipped with spongelike tissues which make it able to float and thus be spread by sea.

We will just give a brief list of the other dune plants, starting with the *Leguminosae*.

Lotus cytisoides (**126**). Hairy plant with silvery trunk and leaves. Flowers 8-14 mm., clustered in heads of 2-6.

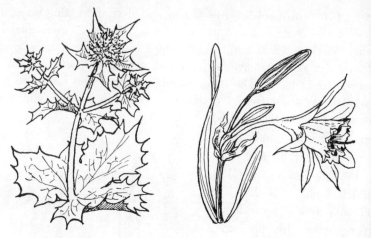

124. *Eryngium maritimum.* Sea holly.
125. *Pancratium maritimum.* Sea daffodil.

Medicago marina - sea medick. Even hairier than the foregoing; stems and leaves almost white. Smaller flowers (6-8 mm.) and grouped in heads of 5-10.

Medicago littoralis. Much less hairy than the two previous plants. Its flowers are even smaller than the foregoing (5-6 mm.) and clustered in heads of 1-6. It is not as common as the two preceding plants.

The three members of the mustard family to be found on beaches are:

Cakile maritima - sea rocket (**127**). A prostrate plant with fleshy leaves, a distinctive fruit in two sections and a violet flower. This plant is only 40-60 cm., tall, but its roots sometimes penetrate as deeply as 2-4 metres into the sand.

Matthiola sinuata - sea stock. An erect plant with many hairy, lobed leaves at the base and fewer on the stem. The flower is also a violet color, but more attractive than that of *Cakile maritima.*

Lobularia maritima - sweet alison. A small plant (10-30 cm.) with small white flowers (sometimes with a slight pink tinge) clustered in round heads. Commonly used as a garden plant. There are many of them around Bellver Castle just outside Palma.

There are also three *Compositae* which grow on the beaches:

Helichrysum stoechas (see p. 112).

Anthemis maritima which the French call dune chamomile, and indeed it is a highly aromatic plant. Its heads are white outside and yellow inside with divided, fleshy leaves dotted with little cavities.

Aetheorhiza (or *Crepis*) *bulbosa*. An ordinary-looking plant, about 20 cm. tall, with a single (rarely two) sow-thistle-like flower. All its leaves are basal and underground it has a tuber the size of a hazel-nut.

Other plants found on the beaches are:

Teucrium capitatum which we have already met (p. 56), and *Teucrium belion* with its white flower (only occasionally pink) and somewhat whiter leaf than the former. When not in flower, both these plants are easy to confuse with *Helichrysum*

126. *Lotus cytisoides.*   127. *Cakile maritima.* Sea rocket.

stoechas, but the *Teucrium* often has clustered leaves and does not have the typical curry smell.

Euphorbia paralias - sea spurge, the most common dune spurge. It has a woody stem 30-60 cm. tall with leaves imbricated against the stem. The other two dune spurges have much more spreading leaves. *Euphorbia terracina* has long (15-40 mm.) narrow, alternate leaves, whilst *Euphorbia peplis* has short (5-20 mm.) opposite leaves and is, furthermore, a small (5-20 cm), prostrate plant.

Calystegia soldanella - sea bindweed, is a member of the *Convulvulaceae* (see p. 75) with leaves that are wider than they are long (rather kidney-shaped) and a pale pink flower with white lines.

A plant that is found more in the sandy terrain along the coast rather than on the beaches themselves is *Glaucium flavum* or yellow horned-poppy. As its common name correctly implies, it is a close relation to the corn poppy (p. 75) with a similar, but yellow, flower, glaucous gray-green leaves and a narrow fruit which may grow as long as 20 cm. or more.

There is also a series of interesting shrubs on our sandy coasts. For purposes of defining an association the most important, as we will see below, is the *Crucianella maritima* (**128**). This is the smallest of our dune shrubs, not generally exceeding a height of 30 cm. It has pointed leaves with white, slightly transparent edges grouped in whorls of four and has small tubular yellow flowers. Not much larger is *Thymelaea myrtifolia* (see p. 85) in its seaside locations at Ca'n Picafort and S'Arenal. The two cistuses of the dunes are the common *Cistus salvifolius,* or sage-leaved cistus, and the much rarer *Cistus clusii* (see p. 38).

It would now be a good idea to classify all these plants according to their natural communities. Closest to the sea we find the *Agropyretum mediterraneum* mainly characterized by:

Elymus farctus ssp. *farctus* (= *Agropyron junceum* ssp. *mediterraneum*)
Sporobolus pungens
Euphorbia peplis

Somewhat further inland we find the *Ammophiletum arundi-naceae* with:

>   *Ammophila arenaria* ssp. *arundinacea*
>   *Medicago marina*

Still further from the sea we find the *Crucianelletum maritimae* with:

Crucianella maritima	*Helichrysum stoechas*
Pancratium maritimum	*Teucrium belion*

 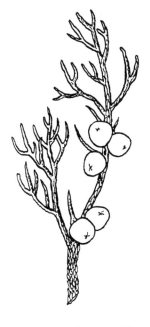

128. *Crucianella maritima.*   129. *Juniperus phoenica.* Phoenician juniper.

All three of these associations are part of the *Ammophilion* alliance of which the following species are most typical in the Balearic Islands:

Eryngium maritimum
Cakile maritima
Matthiola sinuata
Euphorbia paralias

Medicago littoralis
Lotus cytisoides
Calystegia soldanella
Anthemis maritima

with the other plants we have mentioned as their companions.

Behind the *Ammophilion* we find a dune variety of the *Oleo-Ceratonion* (see p. 61) which is characterized by the presence of juniper. On all the beaches of the Balearic Islands, except that of Alcúdia, one finds the Phoenician juniper, *Juniperus phoenicea* var. *lycia* (**129**), with its tiny scale-like leaves pressed against the branches. At the Bay of Alcúdia we find the subspecies *macrocarpa,* always much rarer and localized, of the *Juniperus oxycedrus* (p. 30). It may be distinguished from the normal prickly juniper or cade by its larger leaves and its larger, violet-colored fruit which is pruinose (i. e. with a fine waxy covering like, for example, a grape). These junipers are accompanied, among other plants, by

Pinus halepensis
Pistacia lentiscus
Cistus salvifolius
Phillyrea angustifolia (and on rare occasions, *P. latifolia*)
Asparagus stipularis
Smilax aspera

Before leaving the beaches I would like to go back to the sea a moment to discuss the remnants of dead plants which we find at the water's edge. The famous "seaweed" which piles up on any untended beach, and which is used by farmers to fertilize their fields, is not algae, as many people think, but the shredded leaves of a higher, seed-bearing plant [20] which grows beneath the water at depths of 5-25 metres, *Posidonia oceanica.* Everyone who has been swimming with a mask has seen how it forms large underwater meadows. During winter storms the leaves are

---

[20] It flowers (in April) and occasionally produces fruit, but normally reproduces by means of rhizomes.

torn off and carried onto the beaches. Furthermore, the rhizomes and bases of the leaves are surrounded by fibres which are the remainder of dead, decomposed leaves. These fibres also get torn away and swept up onto the beaches, and, with the action of the waves, eventually form compact balls, which are locally known by the quaint name of *pets de monja* ("nuns' farts").

Posidonia is not the only higher underwater plant to be found on coasts. We also have *Zostera marina* or eel-grass, *Zostera noltii* (= *Z. nana*) and *Cymodocea nodosa,* all of which are smaller and rarer, particularly the last two.

Lagoons and Salt Marshes

The other habitat of hydrophilic or halophilic plants (i.e. plants which have adapted to live with an excess of moisture or salt) is that of lagoons, marshes and salt flats. They are ecologically complex because they range from fresh water zones to true salt beds, from areas which are always flooded to those which are only partially flooded in winter (and even to some which are never flooded at all), from zones of cultivatable soil to the sand of the coastal dunes. They therefore constitute a wide variety of habitats with a series of transition zones. But within this complex, two major areas can be distinguished: fresh water zones occupied by reed-beds, the *Phragmition australis* and zones of damp, salt-impregnated earth, covered with low shrub-like plants measuring one metre or less in height, with fat, fleshy leaves, the *Arthrocnemetum* (or *Salicornietum*) *fruticosi.*

The reed-beds are the home of giant grasses, and particularly the common reed, *Phragmites australis* (= *P. communis*), from which the alliance takes its name. It may grow to a height of 3 metres or more, spreading over impressive expanses of swamplands, creating a sort of impenetrable jungle, an ideal habitat for a multitude of aquatic birds. We must distinguish the common reed from the giant reed or cane, *Arundo donax,* which is cultivated and sub-spontaneous in the Balearic Islands (this is the reed that is found in river beds in other parts of the island). *Arundo* grows even higher (up to 5 metres), has a stronger, thicker trunk (you could never make a fishing rod from *Phragmites*) and a longer spike (40-70 cm.) which is compact and cylindrical (the *Phragmites'* spike is shorter —15-40 cm.— more feathery and normally pennant shaped. The other grass common to damp ground is fiorin or creeping bent-grass, *Agrostis stolonifera*, which grows no higher than 1.5 metres, has a slender stem —still more so at the nodes— and a feathery spike 20 cm. long. A still taller plant —it can grow up to 3 metres high— resembles a grass because of its stem and leaves, but from its odd inflorescence in the shape of a policeman's club, one can see that it belongs to another family (the *Typhaceae*). This is the lesser reedmace, *Typha angustifolia*, ssp. *australis*. The lower part of the inflorescence (the brown part which remains almost all winter) is a mass of female flowers; on the upper part (the part which comes off once the flowering is over, leaving a bit of bare branch) are the male flowers. Mixed with this species, but not as common, is the greater reedmace or cat's-tail, *Typha latifolia* which is easily distinguished from the former by its leaves which are 10-20 mm. wide (while those of the other rarely exceed 8 mm.) and by the fact that the sections of male and female flowers are almost adjacent (while in the other plant they are usually separated by a space of 3-5 cm.

These five plants all reproduce by means of rhizomes (or by stolons which are like rhizomes but above the ground) and that is why they grow into such compact masses. And interlaced among these tall thick masses we find the bellbine or greater bindweed, *Calystegia sepium*, sister of the sea bindweed found in the dunes (p. 118) and cousin of the two field bindweeds (pp. 75-6), with a large (3-5 cm. in diameter) perfectly white flower.

In the other major zone —damp soil partially flooded in winter and with a fairly high salt content —the dominant plants are those of the goosefoot family, *Chenopodiaceae*, one representative of which, the shrubby glasswort, *Arthrocnemum fruticosum* (**130**) (= *Salicornia fruticosa*) has given its name to the association. The plant can be recognized by its height of 3-10 dm., and by its woody stem and fleshy branches which are jointed

n a series of sections (the flowers, as in the case of all members
)f this family, are insignificant). A related plant is also found in
his zone. This is the *Arthrocnemum glaucum* (**131**) (= *Salicor-
iia macrostachya*) which is distinguishable from the former by
ts much shorter sections (in fact, they are shorter than they
ire wide while those of the *fruticosum* are 3-5 times longer than

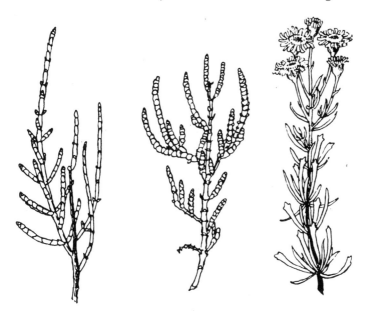

130. *Arthrocnemum fruticosum*. Shrubby glasswort.
131.   ”   *glaucum*.
132. *Inula crithmoides*. Golden samphire.

they are wide). Another member of this family found frequently
in this zone is the sea purslane, *Halimione* (or *Obione*) *portula-
coides,* with opposite, fleshy and silvery leaves, and which in
August or September produces spikes of tiny greenish white
flowers at the tips of its vertical branches.

The other family represented in the *Arthrocnemetum fruticosum* is the *Compositae*. The most ubiquitous is golden samphire, *Inula crithmoides* (**132**), related to *Dittrichia* (or *Inula*)
viscosa (p. 66), which is also found in these areas. The flower

of *crithmoides* is identical to that of the *viscosa* but with a slightly deeper orange centre. The leaves, however, are completely different: narrow, fleshy, widening gradually from the base to the apex and often ending in three small teeth. The *Aster tripolium*, sea aster, also has fleshy leaves, but they are wider and flatter; and its flower has a yellow-orange center and is purplish white on the outside. The leaves of *Artemisia gallica* (or *A. caerulescens* ssp. *gallica* as it is now called) are slightly fleshy and laciniate (except for the upper leaves which are usually entire). This is a very aromatic plant, sister to the *Artemisia absinthium*, or wormwood, used in medicine and, in France, to produce the famous absinthe. *A. gallica* has a grey stem, somewhat greyish leaves and flowers shaped like little closed buttons, measuring 3-4 mm. in diameter.

The reader will have noted that all these plants of a salty environment have more or less fleshy leaves. This is because, through the semi-permeable tissues of the roots, water is always diffused towards the side with the highest salt content (in order to keep both sides balanced). In such a salty environment a normal plant would immediately lose all its water, wilt and die. In order to combat this, halophytes have a high osmotic pressure (for example, osmotic pressures of 40-80 atmospheres have been measured in *Arthrocnemum glaucum*). This high osmotic pressure swells the plant cells, thus producing the fleshiness of its tissues.

Within the two environments of fresh and salt water, there are two families, the rushes and sedges, the members of which are difficult to identify without going into technical details which would be inappropriate here. Therefore I shall simply list the most common representatives and would advise the reader who wants to identify them to consult Polunin's book on the *Flowers of Europe* (which has excellent photographs) or Fournier's flora (see Bibliography).

Juncaceae (rushes)

Juncus acutus	*Juncus effusus*
Juncus bufonius	*Juncus maritimus*

Cyperaceae (sedges)

Scirpus maritimus
Scirpus littoralis
Scirpus holoschoenus

Schoenus nigricans
Carex extensa
Cladium mariscus

It is worth noting that the *Scirpus holoschoenus* (= *Holoschoenus vulgaris*) of the second list is the club-rush commonly found near springs and other damp places in the interior of Majorca.

We cannot leave these halophilic areas without mentioning the only trees (apart from the pine) to be found there: the tamarisks. There are three main species in the Balearic Islands: *Tamarix africana* mostly limited to the bay of Alcúdia, *Tamarix canariensis* commoner on the south of the island, and *Tamarix gallica* mixed in with the former. Recently (1979) an African species, *Tamarix boveana*, was discovered in the Bay of Alcúdia. They are difficult to tell apart, but they are all lovely trees with a shiny blackish-red bark and feathery leaves.

These trees complete our list of the most common wild plants of the Balearic Islands, those most likely to arouse the curiosity of the nature lover. But, as we said in the introduction, they are only a few of the more than fifteen hundred plants to be found in our islands. The reader who wants to begin identifying more plants and acquiring a more thorough knowledge of our botany will find a list of useful books on the following pages.

BIBLIOGRAPHY

A. Books for the novice, with abundant photographs and drawings.

1. O. POLUNIN and A. HUXLEY. *Flowers of the Mediterranean,* London, 1975. Excellent introduction to the most typically Mediterranean flora.

2. O. POLUNIN, *Flowers of Europe,* London, 1969. Excellent complement to the foregoing, with many plants which are not strictly Mediterranean, but which are to be found in the fields, along the roads, and on the coasts of the Balearic Islands.

3. O. POLUNIN and B.E. SMYTHIES, *Flowers of South-West Europe, a field guide,* London, 1973. A complement to the two aforementioned volumes, dedicated solely to the Iberian Peninsula, the south of France and the Balearic Islands. Interesting, but not as useful for the novice as the other two.

4. E. GUINEA, *Flora básica,* Madrid, 1961. Only a limited selection, but useful to the beginner because of its abundant illustrations.

B. For the person wishing to begin to work with botanical keys:

5. P. FOURNIER, *Les quatre flores de la France,* Paris, 1961. Very schematic but highly informative drawings of each plant. Complete for France and Corsica (and thus contains our Tyrrhenian species). One of the books most highly recommended for the beginner who wishes to start seriously working with botanical classification.

6. G. BONNIER, *Flore complète portative de la France, de la Suisse et de la Belgique,* Paris, undated. It is not as complete as the title would lead you to believe, nor is

it particularly trustworthy, but it is a good aid to the novice wanting to overcome the problems of using botanical keys. It has numerous illustrations of the flora details used in classification and is thus highly useful but *only as a complement* to no. 5.

These last two books make no mention whatever of Balearic flora which is of more restricted or southerly distribution (endemic, Ibero-mauritanian species, etc.) and the first four books only mention it sporadically. For a complete idea of the flora of the Balearic Islands the reader will be obliged to consult books within one of the following categories:

C. Floras of more general areas, but including the Balearic Islands.

7. T. G. TUTIN et al., *Flora Europaea*, 5 vols., Cambridge, 1964-80. A reference work of the highest scientific quality, with keys but no illustrations. Essential for the serious botanist, but too technical and difficult for the beginner.

8. A *Flora* of Catalonia, Valencia and the Balearic Islands by ORIOL DE BOLÒS is now in press. Because of the author's prestige and his knowledge of the flora of the islands (see nos. 19 and 20 below), this book will also be indispensable.

D. Floras of the Balearic Islands.

9. P. MARÈS and G. VIGINEIX, *Catalogue raisonné des plantes vasculaires des îles Baléares*, Paris, 1880. A good *flora* which had the misfortune to be overshadowed, almost as soon as it was published, by the book listed immediately below. At the end of the book there are ten marvellous engravings of endemic plants.

10. F. BARCELÓ Y COMBIS, *Flora de las Islas Baleares*, Palma, 1879-1881, and recent reedition in offset, but without publisher's name. A remarkable book for its time, with a description of every species (but no illustrations).

11. H. KNOCHE, *Flora balearica*, Montpellier, 1921-23 (recently reprinted in Holland). Four volumes: the first two

constitute a flora; the third is an overview of the vegetation of the Balearic Islands (climate, history, associations, etc.) with a very complete bibliography of earlier works; the fourth contains a very interesting series of photographs of landscapes and plants. This is one of most complete works on the flora of the Balearic Islands in existence, but it is difficult to use. It has no key and gives no descriptions and its system of localizing species is extraordinarily complicated and imprecise. Furthermore, the author sometimes gives the impression of wanting to reorganize the entire field of botanical taxonomy, using the Balearic flora as his weapon, with the result that the poor reader is trapped in confusion on the battlefield. Nonetheless it is an indispensable reference book for anyone who wants to make a thorough study of the botany of the Balearic Islands.

12. J. Duvigneaud, *Catalogue provisoire de la flore des Baléares*, Liège (Belgium), 2nd ed., 1979. A simple catalogue which lists each species, the islands on which it is found and whether or not it is endemic. It is very up-to-date, written with great authority (by the discoverer of *Naufraga balearica*) and exceedingly useful.

12a. A. Hansen, *Checklist of the Vascular Plants of the Balearic Islands (Mallorca, Menorca, Ibiza, Formentera)*, Copenhagen, 1974. Similar to the Duvigneaud catalogue, but without the distribution by islands. Also useful.

E. Floras of specific islands:

13. Majorca:

F. Bonafè, *Flora de Mallorca*, 4 vols., Palma, 1977-80. An exceptionally complete work, with a description of each species and an abundance of photographs. A must for both amateur and professional botanists.

14. Minorca:

a) J. J. Rodríguez Femenías, *Flórula de Menorca,* Mahon, 1904. A new edition of this classic work is being prepared by M. A. Cardona and L. Llorens.

b) M. A. Cardona, the section on *Botànica* in the *Enciclopèdia de Menorca*. At present (1981) only the

9

part on the lower plants has appeared; but when complete should constitute an excellent survey of the Minorcan flora. The same author has also brought out a good *Estudi de les zones d'interès botànic i ecològic de Menorca,* published by the Consell Insular de Menorca, 1980.

15. There is no single volume dedicated to the plants of Ibiza, only two partial studies:

a) P. FONT I QUER, *La flora de las Pitiusas y sus afinidades con la de la península ibérica,* Barcelona, 1927 (in "Memorias de la Real Academia de Ciencias y Artes de Barcelona", Tercera Epoca, vol. XX, Núm. 4).

b) *Aportació inicial al coneixement de les plantes d'Eivissa i Formentera* compiled by the students of Natural Sciencies of the Institute of Ibiza and published by the Institut d'Estudis Eivissencs, Ibiza, 1974. A good example of what an intelligent and enterprising teacher (in this case, Guerau d'Arellano i Tur) can get out of a group of students. The work discusses only 36 species, but they are well-chosen and described, with illustrations, photographs and distribution maps, and with notes on uses and customs. A new and enlarged edition —called *Nova aportació al coneixement...* —has just (1981) appeared, done in collaboration with Nestor Torres and with drawings by Josep Escandell.

16. There are two studies on the island of Cabrera:

a) A. MARCOS, *Contribució al coneixement de la flora balear. Flòrula de Cabrera i dels illots pròxims,* in "Cavanillesia", Vol. VIII, pp. 1-52, 1936.

b) P. PALAU I FERRER, *Catàleg de la flòrula de l'illa de Cabrera i dels illots que l'envolten,* finished in 1954, and finally published along with *Impressions sobre la vegetació de l'illa de Cabrera* by O. de Bolòs and a group of collaborators in *Treballs de la Institució Catalana d'Història Natural* N.º 7, Barcelona, 1976.

'. General overviews of the flora of the Balearic Islands:

17. Mlle. L. CHODAT, *Contribution à la géobotanique de Majorque*. Thesis, Inst. Botanique de Geneve, 1924. Difficult to locate, but very interesting.

18. G. COLOM, *Biogeografía de las Baleares*, Palma, 1957 and *El medio y la vida en las Baleares*, Palma, 1964. Of limited botanical interest, but with good illustrations. The former contains an excellent bibliography.

19. ORIOL DE BOLÒS and R. MOLINIER, *Recherches phytoso-ciologiques dans l'ille de Majorque*, in "Collectanea Botanica", Vol. V, separata III, Barcelona, 1958. A work of major importance which eliminates the need to consult many of the aforementioned works (for example, a large part of Vol. III of Knoche) and which has served as a basis for this book of mine. The same authors in collaboration with P. MONTSERRAT, have also published *Observations phytosociologiques dans l'île de Minorque* in "Acta Geobotanica Barcinonensia". Vol. 5, 1970 which is excellent and every bit as indispensable as the former. A similar study by the same authors on Ibiza is due to appear shortly in English in *Monographiae Biologicae* published in The Hague. For Cabrera, see the *Impressions...* mentioned in 16b above.

19.ª R. FOLCH I GUILLÈN, *La vegetació dels països catalans*, Barcelona, 1981. A superb and remarkably complete survey of the plant communities in the area extending from Perpignan and Andorra down to Alicante, and including the Balearic Islands (the area in which the Catalan language is spoken).

20. ORIOL DE BOLÒS, *Grupos corológicos de la flora balear*, in "Publ. Inst. Biol. Apl." XXVII, pp. 45-71, Barcelona, 1958. Important overview of the distribution of our species.

21. J. DUVIGNEAUD, *Excursion du 21 au 28 Juin 1974 à Majorque. Syllabus introductif*, Liège (Belgium), 1974. A good introduction to Balearic botany, prepared for a trip the author made with his students. A good part of the material contained therein was published in the journal "Les Naturalistes Belges" of October, 1967 (Vol. 48, n.º 8).

G.   Miscellaneous bibliography:

22.   There is a large number of important articles by C. PAU
S. GARCIAS FONT, Brother BIANOR, FONT QUER, P. MONT
SERRAT, PALAU FERRER, Father CAÑIGUERAL, O. DE BOLÒS
S. PIGNATTI, G. ORELL, L. LLORENS, M. A. CARDONA and
others, referring to the Balearic Islands in journals such
as "Butlletí de l'Institució Catalana d'Història Natural"
"Collectanea Botanica" (both of Barcelona), "Anales de
Instituto Botánico Cavanilles" (of Madrid) and "Boletín
de la Sociedad de Historia Natural de Baleares". For
these articles and other works, see the bibliographies contained in nos. 11, 13, 18, 19 and 20 above. For keeping
up with recent bibliography, the brief reviews in the
last-named journal are especially helpful. For recent con-
tributions which will help bring the reader up to date,
I suggest L. LLORENS, *Nueva contribución al conoci-
miento de la flora Balear* in "Mediterránea" (Alicante)
3 (1979), pp. 101-122, and M. A. CARDONA, *Consideracions
sobre l'endemisme i l'origen de la flora de les illes balears*
in "Buttletí de la Inst. Cat. d'Hist. Nat." 44, Botànica 3
(1979), pp. 7-15, both as overviews and for their bibliographies, as well as the last-named author's "Endemism
and Evolution in the Islands of the Western Mediterranean," published in *Plants and Islands*, London, 1979,
pp. 133-169.

H.   Classic Floras of surrounding countries; reference works
which are often very useful to the specialist:

23.   For France there are the works of COSTE and ROUY; for
Corsica the work of BRIQUET; for Italy the work of FIORI,
and for Spain, the work of WILLKOMM. For North Africa
—very important for the Balearic Islands— there is the
monumental work by MAIRE which is in the process of
being published. Furthermore, there is JAHANDIEZ and
MAIRE's work on Morocco and QUEZEL and SANTA's work
on Algeria. For specific references, see the bibliographies
contained in nos. 1, 2, 3 and 7 on this list. For the
English-speaking reader, a particularly useful book is
S. M. HASLAM et al., *A Flora of the Maltese Islands,* Malta
University Press, 1977. It includes many species found
in the Balearic Islands, with good keys, accurate descriptions in English, and an illustration of each genus.

. Medicinal plants:

24. P. PALAU FERRER, *Les plantes medicinals baleàriques*,
    Palma, 1954; new edition, 1981, in this same series.
    Written by an apothecary and botanist, this is an excep-
    tionally interesting little book.

J. On ecology and conservation:

25. There is the recent and excellent *Natura, ús o abús?*
    Llibre blanc de la Gestió de la Natura als Països Cata-
    lans, published by the Institució Catalana d'Història Na-
    tural and edited by RAMON FOLCH I GUILLEN.

ÍNDEX

INDEX OF SCIENTIFIC NAMES

With the exception of the photographs, all numbers refer to pages. Those with a drawing of the plant are in boldface, and those with a map are in italics.

Ophrys tenthredinifera, sawfly orchid, 50, **51**, 52, 62
Orchis coriophora, bug orchid, **51**, 52
Orchis laxiflora ssp. *palustris*, 53 n. 8
Orchis longibracteata, see *Barlia robertiana*
Orchis longicornu, long-spurred orchid, **51**, 52
Orchis mascula, early purple orchid, **51**, 52
Orchis tridentata, toothed orchid, **51**, 52-3
Orzyzopsis miliacea, see *Piptatherum miliaceum*
Osyris alba, 32, **33**, 107
Osyris quadripartita, 32
Oxalis pes-caprae (= *O. cernua*), Cape sorrel, Bermuda buttercup, 75, **75**

Paeonia cambessedessii, peony, 83, Photo 5
Pallenis spinosa, 66, **67**
Pancratium maritimum, sea daffodil, 115, **116**, 119
Papaver dubium, 75
Papaver hybridum, 75
Papaver rhoeas, common poppy, 75
Papaver somniferum, opium poppy, 75
Papilionaceae (= *Lotoideae*), 33, 54, 77-8, 83-4
Pastinaca lucida, 82, **82**, 83
Pastinaca sativa, wild parsnip, 82
Pastinacetum lucidae, 83
Phagnalon rupestre, 97
Phagnalon saxatile, 97
Phagnalon sordidum, 97
Phillyrea angustifolia, 27, **27**, 62, 120
Phillyrea latifolia, 27, **27**, 61, 120
Phillyrea media, 27 n. 4; var. *rodriguezii*, 113, **113**, 114
Phlomis italica, 85, **86**
Phragmites australis (= *P. communis*), common reed, 121
Phragmition australis, 121
Phyllitis sagittata (= *Scolopendrium hemionitis*), **95**, 96
Phyllitis scolopendrium (= *Scolopendrium vulgare, S. officinale*), 96
Pimpinella anisum, anise, 102
Pimpinella bicknelli (= *Spiroceratium bicknelli, Adarianta bicknelli*), 102, 113
Pimpinella tragium var. *balearica*, 91, 93
Pinus halepensis, Aleppo pine, *13*, 17, 18, 22, 62, 63, 120; var. *ceciliae*, 18

Pinus pinea, umbrella pine, stone pine, 18
Piptatherum miliaceum (= *Oryzopsis miliacea*), **73**, 74
Pistacia lentiscus, mastic tree, lentiak, 19, 22, 24, 62, 64, 120
Pistacia terebinthus, turpentine tree, 24
Pistacia vera, pistachio, 24
Plantaginaceae, plantain family, 79
Platanus orientalis, London plane, 105, **106**
Pleurotus eryngii, 59
Poa annua, annual meadow-grass, **73**, 74
Polypodium australe, **95**, 96
Populus alba, white poplar, 105, **106**
Populus nigra, black poplar, 105, **106**
Posidonia oceanica, 120
Potentilla caulescens, 91, 93, 107
Potentilla reptans, creeping cinquefoil, 107
Potentillo-Pimpinelletum balearicum, 93
Primula vulgaris ssp. *balearica*, white primrose, 93, Photo 20
Prunus spinosa, blackthorn, 105
Psoralea bituminosa, pitch trefoil, 55, **56**
Pteridium aquilinum, bracken, **59**, 60

Quercetalia ilicis, 60, 62
Quercetea ilicis, 60
Quercion ilicis, oak forest, 14, 60, 61, 63, 64
Quercus coccifera, kermes oak, 15, 17, 64
Quercus faginea (= *Q. lusitanica* ssp. *valentina*), Lusitanian oak, 16, 17, **106**
Quercus ilex, *13*, 14, 17, 22, 61
Quercus lusitanica ssp. *valentina*, see *Q. faginea*
Quercus rotundifolia, 15, 17
Quercus suber, cork oak, 16

Ranunculus ficaria ssp. *ficariiformis*, lesser celandine, 107
Ranunculus weyleri, 101
Raphanus raphanistrum, wild radish, 72
Raphanus sativus, cultivated radish, 72
Reichardia picroides, 68, 112
Reseda alba, white mignonette, 78
Reseda lutea, wild mignonette, 78
Reseda luteola, dyer's rocket, 78

Ulmus minor, smooth-leaved elm, 105, **106**
Umbelliferae, 69-71, 91, 102
Umbilicus horizontalis, pennywort, 96
Urginea maritima (= *Scilla maritima*), sea squill, 87
Urospermum dalechampii, 67, **68**
Urospermum picroides, 67
Urtica atrovirens ssp. *bianorii,* 101

Viburnum tinus, laurustinus, 100
Vicia bifoliolata, 8, 103
Vinca difformis, periwinkle, 107
Viola jaubertiana, 100, Photo 6
Vitex agnus-castus, chaste tree, 107

Zostera marina, eel grass, 121
Zostera noltii (= *Z. nana*), 121

INDEX OF ENGLISH NAMES

garlic — *Allium*
geranium family — *Geraniaceae*
germander, wall — *Teucrium chamaedrys*
gladiolus — *Gladiolus*
glasswort, shrubby — *Arthrocnemun fruticosum*
globularia, shrubby — *Globularia alypum*
goosefoot family — *Chenopodiaceae*
grass family — *Gramineae*
grass, annual meadow — *Poa annua*
grass, Bermuda — *Cynodon dactylon*
grass, creeping bent — *Agrostis stolonifera*
grass, eel — *Zostera marina*
grass, esparto — *Stipa tenacissima*
grass, marram — *Ammophila arenaria* ssp. *arundinacea*
grass, sea-fern — *Desmazeria marina*

hare's-tail — *Lagurus ovatus*
hawthorn — *Crataegus monogyna* ssp. *brevispina*
heather family — *Ericaceae*
heather, green — *Erica scoparia*
heather, tree — *Erica arborea*
hellebore, stinking — *Helleborus foetidus* var. *balearicus*
hemlock — *Conium maculatum*
holly — *Ilex aquifolium* f. *balearica*
holly, sea — *Eryngium maritimum*
honeysuckle — *Lonicera implexa*
hyacinth, grape — *Muscari neglectum*
hyacinth, tassel — *Muscari comosum*

inula, aromatic — *Dittrichia viscosa*
ivy — *Hedera helix*

joint-pine — *Ephedra fragilis*
Judas tree — *Cercis siliquastrum*
juniper, prickly — *Juniperus oxycedrus*

laurel — *Laurus nobilis*
laurustinus — *Viburnum tinus*
lavender, French — *Lavandula stoechas*
lavender, toothed — *Lavandula dentata*
leek, wild — *Allium ampeloprasum*
lentisk — *Pistacia lentiscus*
lily family — *Liliaceae*
madder wild — *Rubia peregrina*

mallow family — *Malvaceae*
marigold, field — *Calendula arvensis*
marigold, garden — *Calendula officinalis*
mastic tree — *Pistacia lentiscus*
meadow-grass, annual — *Poa annua*
medick, sea — *Medicago marina*
mezereon, Mediterranean — *Daphne gnidium*
mespilus, snowy — *Amelanchier ovalis*
mignonette — *Reseda*
mint family — *Labiatae*
mustard family — *Cruciferae*
mustard, hedge — *Sisymbrium officinale*
mustard, white — *Sinapis alba*
myrtle — *Myrtus communis*

oak, cork — *Quercus suber*
oak, holm — *Quercus ilex*
oak, kermes — *Quercus coccifera*
oak, lusitanian — *Quercus faginea*
oats — *Avena*
oleander — *Nerium oleander*
olive — *Olea europea*
orchid, bee — *Ophrys apifera*
orchid, brown bee — *Ophrys fusca*
orchid, bug — *Orchis coriophora*
orchid, bumble-bee — *Ophrys bombyliflora*
orchid, early purple — *Orchis mascula*
orchid, early spider — *Ophrys sphegodes*
orchid, long-spurred — *Orchis longicornu*
orchid, mirror — *Ophrys speculum*
orchid, pyramidal — *Anacamptis pyramidalis*
orchid, sawfly — *Ophrys tenthredinifera*
orchid, tongue — *Serapias lingua*
orchid, toothed — *Orchis tridentata*

palm, dwarf fan — *Chamaerops humilis*
parsnip, wild — *Pastinaca sativa*
pea family — *Leguminosae*
pennywort — *Umbilicus horizontalis*
peony — *Paeonia cambessedesii*
periwinkle — *Vinca difformis*
pimpernel, scarlet — *Anagallis arvensis*
pine, Aleppo — *Pinus halepensis*
pine, stone — *Pinus pinea*

TABLE OF CONTENTS